641.5
1:1

T

VERY
BASIC
COOKBOOK

0 11557 03280 2

NOV 0 2 2006

Published by
STACKPOLE BOOKS
5067 Ritter Rd.
Mechanicsburg PA 17055
www.stackpolebooks.com
© Stackpole Books 2005

First published in 2005 by
Lansdowne Publishing Pty Ltd

Created and produced by Lansdowne Publishing Pty Ltd
© Copyright text, photography and design: Lansdowne Publishing Pty Ltd 2005
www.lansdownepublishing.com.au. Email: sales@lanspub.com.au

Printed in Singapore

10 9 8 7 6 5 4 3 2 1

First edition

Library of Congress Cataloging-in-Publication Data
on file with the Library of Congress

ISBN 0-8117-3280-2

THE
VERY
BASIC
COOKBOOK

Vicki Liley

STACKPOLE
BOOKS

Contents

Meat 38

Purchasing meat • Storing meat • Freezing guide • Meat cooking methods: How to barbecue, pan grill, broil (grill); How to make a casserole or stew; How to panfry; How to stir-fry; How to roast; How to rest a roast; How to serve a hot roast dinner • Basic roast beef • Roast meat gravy • Basic roast lamb with potatoes • Mint sauce • Applesauce for basic roast pork • Basic roast pork • Beef casserole • Beef and noodle stir-fry • Chili con carne • Cottage pie • Panfried steak with garlic butter • Hamburgers • Osso buco • Gremolata • Steak sandwich with caramelized onions • Tomato, prosciutto and olive pizza • Warm Thai beef salad

Chicken 58

Purchasing chicken • Storing chicken • Chicken cooking methods: How to prepare chicken for cooking; How to test chicken for doneness; How to rest a roast chicken • Basic roast chicken • Roast chicken gravy • Roast chicken with herb stuffing • Panfried chicken fillet with green peppercorn sauce • Chicken and cashew stir-fry • Chicken cacciatore • Chicken in red wine with mushrooms • Honey-soy chicken wings

Fish 68

Purchasing fish • Storing fish • Freezing fresh fish • Fish cooking methods: How to barbecue or pan grill fish; How to bake fish; How to deep-fry fish; How to broil (grill) fish; How to panfry fish; How to poach fish; How to steam fish; How to test if fish is cooked • Baked and seasoned whole fish • Fish cakes • Fish curry • Panfried fish with tartar sauce • Tartar sauce

Salads and side breads 78

Purchasing salad ingredients • Storing salad ingredients • How to prepare salad ingredients; How to refresh salad leaves • Basic salad dressings: French dressing; Italian dressing; Balsamic vinegar dressing; Basic mayonnaise • Caesar salad • Chef's salad • Greek salad • Green salad • Potato salad • Salade niçoise • Tabbouleh • Waldorf salad • Warm penne and tomato salad • Herb-garlic bread • Tomato bruschette

Pasta 94

Pasta cooking methods: Recommended servings for pasta; How to cook fresh pasta; How to cook dried pasta; How to test if pasta is al dente; How to drain cooked pasta; How to serve pasta; How to reheat cooked pasta; How to store cooked pasta • Basic bolognese sauce • Spaghetti bolognese • Beef and ricotta lasagna • Fettuccine carbonara • Macaroni and cheese • Neapolitan sauce • Pesto sauce • Spaghetti with olive oil and garlic sauce • Spaghetti and meatballs

Rice, noodles, lentils and couscous 106

Cooking methods: How to cook rice; How to cook couscous; How to cook noodles; How to cook lentils • Basic risotto • Couscous salad • Fried rice • Lentil and bacon stew • Lentil patties • Pad Thai noodles • Tomato and tuna risotto

Vegetables 116

Purchasing vegetables • Storing vegetables • Vegetable cooking methods: How to blanch vegetables; How to barbecue or pan grill vegetables; How to mash vegetables; How to puree vegetables;

How to roast vegetables; How to stir-fry vegetables; How to boil or steam vegetables; Quick reference guide to boiling and steaming vegetables • Asparagus with easy hollandaise sauce • Classic hollandaise sauce • Cauliflower au gratin • Creamy mashed potatoes • Crispy roast potatoes • Hash brown potatoes • Guacamole • Oven-roasted vegetable salad • Potato, ham and cheese bake • Ratatouille • Slow-roasted tomatoes • Stir-fried Asian vegetables • Stuffed mushrooms • Vegetable lasagna

Introduction

About 30 years ago, when I started high school, I began my love affair with cooking. In those days, everyone (even the boys) would study home economics as a compulsory subject. I still remember the first lesson: we learned to boil, poach and scramble eggs, then we made sandwiches filled with our cooked eggs. Now I realize it was home economics that gave me a foundation in, and invaluable understanding of, a balanced diet, food preparation skills and cooking techniques—the basics.

Since those first tentative days in the school kitchen, I have continued to apply the basic principles that I learned. They've taken me a long way in the food industry, and every time I cook I call on those skills, most often without realizing it. Which is how this book came about. A gap has developed— home economics is no longer compulsory, life is hectic and time is short, and convenience foods have reduced the need to cook at home. Many of the basics have been forgotten, or were never known.

A basic understanding of food and cooking techniques is the key to great things in the kitchen. It also helps you to maintain a healthy and balanced diet for yourself and your family, and is economical, saving you time and money. With just a few basic skills, you will be able to cook anything your taste buds desire. And the enjoyment of transforming raw ingredients into something deliciously satisfying cannot be compared.

The recipes in this book are a collection of my favorite basics. They have been chosen because they are simple, delicious, and have stood the test of time. Some, like macaroni and cheese and cottage pie, are instantly recognizable as the all-time greats your grandmother and mother used to make. These were quite often invented with the family budget in mind but have also adapted to our modern kitchens. Others, such as hamburgers and pasta salads, are contemporary classics that have evolved as a result of our fast-paced lives. All the recipes utilize the basic techniques of home cooking, and they're easy to make, mostly using commonly available ingredients from the supermarket.

In addition to recipes, you'll find step-by-step information on the basic cooking techniques, from peeling tomatoes or stir-frying to melting chocolate. There are also lots of hints and ideas to guide you. With these skills in your kitchen repertoire, you'll be able to approach cooking with a sense of adventure and fun—and nothing will ever seem too hard to cook again.

Most of all, this book encourages you to enjoy the magic of cooking. Once you've got the basics, you can get creative. Start with some of these recipes, then refine and adapt them to your own experience, style and taste. Shop around and experiment with ingredients, get inspired. Use this book as a guide, a friend in the kitchen. If the recipes aren't already your personal favorites, I hope one day they will be.

Happy cooking!

Ingredients

Basic pantry items

Your food pantry is much like your clothes closet—you need these places to exist, but you also go there to seek inspiration and comfort from the items within. On cold and windy days, you might grab the ingredients for a heartwarming stew from the pantry, just as you grab a warm coat and scarf from the closet. In summer you might choose a big shady hat and light clothes, and ingredients for a cooling salad or an outdoor barbecue.

Your pantry needs to be stocked with essential items for all seasons, but should also continually inspire you to create balanced and nutritious meals. A well-stocked pantry is indeed an asset when you can't get to the store, it's cold and rainy outside, your favorite movie is on television, or unexpected guests drop in for dinner.

Your pantry, like your closet, says a lot about your life. Mine is a tiny cupboard, but friends say it's like a gourmet supermarket, and they get hungry just peeking inside! There's all manner of bottles, huge jars of rice, row upon row of containers, stacks of cans—of tomatoes, chickpeas, and of course tuna (too many to count!)—collections of dried herbs and spices, and a tub of sea salt and a pepper mill that always seem to need refilling. There's also the essential large jar of honey, for my tea.

One shelf is dedicated solely to pasta, rice and noodles—these are among my favorite foods and I love having a variety at my fingertips. Another shelf is home to sauces, with various bottles of soy sauce and fish sauce, vinegars and oils (including quite a collection of olive). For emergencies I keep some good-quality ready-made stock. The top shelves house the baking staples, such as sugar and flour, while the bottom shelves are ideal for baskets of vegetables like pumpkins, onions and garlic.

However, while you could survive on food from your well-stocked pantry alone, it is better for your health and a lot more exciting for your taste buds to include fresh ingredients wherever possible. Fresh fruit, vegetables, bread, dairy products, meat, chicken and fish provide essential vitamins and minerals to help maintain a healthy body, as well as bringing variety to your diet. So whenever possible, eat fresh.

Most importantly, choose quality ingredients whether you're filling your pantry or buying fresh. If you use produce in season and high-quality ingredients, and follow the basic cooking techniques in this book, you can't fail.

Basic pantry list

Here is a list of the items that I consider to be essential in a pantry. Whether you're setting up a pantry or just spring-cleaning, this list will help you establish a workable stock of basic ingredients for creative cooking.

- baking powder
- baking soda (bicarbonate of soda)
- bread crumbs
- canned tomatoes—both whole and crushed
- canned tuna in olive oil—choose a good-quality product
- cooking chocolate—choose a good-quality product
- cornstarch (cornflour)
- dried herbs—oregano, rosemary, thyme; for when you can't get fresh
- fish sauce—choose an Asian-made product for best flavor
- flour—all-purpose (plain), self-rising (self-raising)
- honey
- jam
- lentils—choose organic red and brown lentils if available, for their superior flavor and quality
- mustard—Dijon and whole-grain prepared and dry mustard (mustard powder)
- noodles—cellophane (bean thread), egg, rice; purchase from Asian grocers and markets for better selection and prices
- nuts—pine nuts or almonds are great standbys
- olive oil—I keep a range, from standard or virgin olive oil for cooking to high-quality extra virgin olive oil for drizzling
- olives—good-quality green or black
- pasta—keep a range of types; dried lasagna sheets are handy too
- peppercorns—for the pepper mill
- rice—long-grain white (including basmati and jasmine), short-grain white, Arborio (for risotto)
- sea salt—choose a good-quality product
- soy sauce—purchase a large bottle at the Asian supermarket; light soy sauce is suitable for all-purpose Asian cooking
- spices—ground cumin, cinnamon and coriander are basics, but a wider selection is handy to have
- stock—chicken, beef, vegetable; choose a good-quality product
- sugar—granulated, brown, superfine (caster), confectioners' (icing)
- Thai sweet chili sauce—great as a dip or marinade; purchase an Asian-made product for best flavor

- tomato paste—choose small cartons or tubes rather than large jars; once opened, refrigerate with a layer of olive oil poured over the surface
- vanilla extract (essence)
- vegetable oil—for frying
- vinegars—balsamic, cider, white wine; select a good quality; like wine, the older it is the better it tastes

Preparing a weekly shopping list

Knowing what to buy will halve your cooking efforts, so it's well worth being organized. Here are some hints for successful food shopping:

- First, take the time to plan your weekly menu by setting budgets for money and time. That is, how much money can you spend, and how much time do you have available to cook.
- Think about the meals you wish to prepare, remembering to work within your budgeted time and money. Plan meals based on fresh produce in season, but also take advantage of prepared foods (though these tend to be more expensive) for convenience or if you know you've got a busy week ahead. For example, a good-quality pasta sauce can be enhanced with some fresh herbs and black olives, served over al dente pasta, with green salad and crusty bread.
- Place a notepad or blackboard in your kitchen so that you can make an ongoing shopping list. Jot down items, especially essentials, as you need them.
- Write your shopping list for the week, including any items on the kitchen notepad or blackboard. Aim to include a balance of meat, fish, chicken, breads, grains, fruits and vegetables, fats and oils, and dairy foods. Double check your pantry, refrigerator and freezer: exclude items you already have, and include anything you need.
- Remember to take the shopping list with you when you go shopping!
- Avoid grocery shopping when you are hungry or bored, as this triggers impulsive junk-food purchases.
- Look for supermarket specials, and stock up on essential pantry items if discounted.
- Check use-by dates on perishables such as milk, eggs, yogurt and cheese.
- Only buy the fresh meat, chicken, fish, vegetables and other perishables that you will consume within their optimum period, usually 1–2 days. Or plan to freeze perishables instead.
- When shopping, leave meat, chicken, fish and other perishables until last, so that they remain chilled while you get your purchases home. In hot weather, use an insulated cooler (eski) for perishable products.

Basic equipment for your kitchen

Sometimes, it's easy to think we need every gadget ever invented for the kitchen, and we end up with equipment we never use because it's more work to put it together and to wash it than to do the task by hand. I have a juicer like that—by the time I build it, make the juice, then clean the filter and nozzle, I could have gone out and bought a freshly made juice, twice! So buyer beware: listen to the advice of family and friends about what's good and what's not, and don't be fooled by catchy advertising claims.

The basic equipment is really all you need for most cooking. Kitchen utensils should be easy to use, wash and store. Whenever possible, buy quality, as the equipment will last longer. For example, stainless steel, though more expensive, is more durable than plastic. Kitchenware stores are excellent places to start, as they will stock a wide range of quality items for your kitchen and also offer good advice.

Basic equipment list

The following list includes the basic equipment that will help you create a workable kitchen environment.

- baking and roasting pans—various sizes, preferably nonstick; make sure they fit into your oven
- baking dishes—various sizes; a large dish with lid is handy for stews braised in the oven and casseroles
- cake pans—various shapes and sizes, such as 8-in (20-cm) round and 9-in (23-cm) springform; preferably nonstick
- cutting boards—various sizes and types; I prefer wooden boards, as they don't blunt your knives like plastic ones do
- colander—stainless steel or enamel, with a long handle or handles, for draining pasta and vegetables
- electric mixer—handheld type or countertop mixer, depending on your budget and mixing requirements; choose a reliable brand
- food processor—choose a reliable brand that's easy to use, clean and store
- frying pan—choose a good-quality, large, heavy-based frying pan with a lid, and a medium-sized nonstick frying pan
- kitchen scale—should be able to measure small and large amounts
- knives—choose a good quality cook's knife, a smaller paring knife, and a serrated bread knife
- measuring cups for dry measures (stainless steel or plastic) and measuring cups with a spout for liquid measures (preferably glass); a set of metal or hard plastic measuring spoons for both dry and liquid measures

- pepper mill—this gets a workout, so choose a good-quality mill and it will last longer
- saucepans—start with three good-quality, heavy-based stainless steel saucepans (small, medium and large) with lids; avoid sets, as you will rarely use all the pans included
- kitchen scissors—for snipping fresh herbs and trimming excess fat from meat and chicken; keep them exclusively for use in the kitchen
- steamer—this should fit your wok or medium saucepan; Asian supermarkets stock inexpensive bamboo steamers; metal steamers and sets are also commonly available
- sieve—stainless steel for straining or draining hot foods; nylon for sifting and straining or draining cold foods; choose to fit your mixing bowl
- vegetable peeler—for peeling vegetables and making Parmesan cheese shavings
- wire whisk—stainless steel is best; small and large sizes are handy but not necessary
- wok—(see below)

A wok in your kitchen

If there was one utensil from my kitchen I couldn't survive without, it would be, without a doubt, my wok! Although usually associated with stir-frying, the wok can be used for almost any cooking method, and for almost any ingredient, whether a recipe is Asian or Western in style. The wok's shape accommodates small or large quantities of ingredients and allows control over how they are cooked. The large cooking surface evenly and efficiently conducts and holds heat, which is why a wok is ideal for stir-frying. It is also easy to use, clean and store—the perfect basic implement.

Selecting a wok

All woks are basically bowl shaped, with gently sloping sides. Traditionally they were made from cast iron, and were therefore quite heavy, but they are now available in many different materials and finishes. Carbon steel or rolled steel and cast iron are among the best materials. Nonstick woks are easy to clean but may not promote browning of foods as well as those made with carbon steel. Other options include stainless steel woks and electric woks, but these may not reach temperatures as high as cast iron or carbon steel. Round-bottomed woks work best on gas stoves, though a wok stand may be necessary to provide stability; choose a stand with large perforations to promote good heat circulation. Flat-bottomed woks are suitable for electric stove tops because they sit directly and securely on the heating element. Woks are also available in a range of sizes. A wok with a 14-in (35-cm) diameter is a versatile size for cooking dishes that yield four to six servings.

How to clean and season a new wok

Woks made from carbon steel or rolled steel, the popular inexpensive types sold in Asian stores, are coated with a thin film of lacquer to prevent them from rusting after manufacturing. The film needs to be removed and the wok must be cleaned and seasoned before it can be used for cooking.

To clean a new wok:
1. Place wok on stove top, fill with cold water and add 2 tablespoons baking soda (bicarbonate of soda). Bring to a boil over high heat and boil rapidly for 15 minutes.
2. Drain water and scrub off the coating with a nylon pad. Be careful because wok will be hot.
3. Rinse and dry the wok. It is now ready to be seasoned.

Carbon steel and cast iron woks require seasoning before use. This creates a smooth surface that prevents food from sticking to it and also prevents the wok from discoloring. You should not need to scrub a seasoned wok with detergent after cooking. Instead, clean with hot water and a sponge or nylon pad, then dry well and rub a thin layer of oil over the inside of the wok (to prevent rust) before storing.

To season a new wok:
1. Place cleaned wok over low heat. Have paper towels and vegetable oil handy.
2. When wok is hot, carefully rub 1 tablespoon oil, using paper towels, all over the inside surface.
3. Repeat process with fresh paper towels until they come away clean, without any trace of color.

Basic food preparation and techniques

How to finely chop an onion

Store onions in a cool, dark, well-ventilated place. Some people believe that storing onions in the refrigerator will prevent you from crying when cutting them.

1. Peel tough outer skin from onion. Leave root end intact to keep onion together while chopping.
2. Cut onion in half lengthwise, cutting through root end. Place half, cut side down, on a cutting board. Holding onion at root end and using a small sharp knife, cut vertically into slices ⅛ inch (3 mm) thick, without cutting through root end.
3. Cut onion horizontally into ⅛ inch (3 mm) slices, again without cutting through root end.
4. Cut onion crosswise, to make finely chopped pieces.
5. Repeat with remaining onion half.

How to crush garlic cloves

When buying garlic, select bulbs that are large, plump, firm and dry, with no sign of green shoots. Store in a cool, dark, well-ventilated place. The intense garlic flavor is released when a clove is crushed or cut. The longer you cook garlic, the milder it gets.

1. Remove clove from garlic bulb, place on a cutting board, and crush gently with side of knife to loosen skin. Peel off skin.
2. To chop with a knife, grasp handle with one hand, place fingers of other hand near tip, and move the knife up and down in a rhythmic motion to chop finely. Sprinkle garlic with a little salt if necessary to prevent garlic from sticking to knife blade. Alternatively, pass the peeled clove through a garlic press (crusher; available at kitchenware stores) and discard any fibers remaining in press.

How to toast nuts

Toasting enhances the flavor of unsalted raw nuts, such as peanuts, almonds, and pine nuts. You do not need oil or butter when toasting nuts, as they contain natural oils.

1. Preheat oven to 350°F (180°C/Gas 4).
2. Spread nuts in a single layer on a baking sheet.
3. Toast until golden, about 5 minutes, stirring nuts halfway through cooking time; do not let nuts burn.
4. Remove from baking sheet and let cool.

HINT Alternatively, place nuts in a nonstick frying pan over medium heat and toast, stirring constantly, until golden. Remove from pan and let cool.

How to prepare fresh asparagus spears
1. Take 1 spear of asparagus at a time and hold near the lower third of the cut end.
2. Bend stalk until it snaps.
3. Discard coarse and woody end portion.

How to prepare fresh strawberries
To remove green hull from top of strawberry, trim using a sharp knife. Or pinch stem between thumb and forefinger and gently pull to remove hull from fruit.

How to measure dry ingredients
The most accurate way to measure dry ingredients is to weigh them using a kitchen scale, but you can also measure in cups or spoons.

To measure dry ingredients using a cup or spoon, loosely fill the cup or spoon and level top with a knife. (Use a spoon to transfer such ingredients as flour to the measuring cup.) Do not heap ingredients or pack tightly unless stated in recipe.

How to measure liquid ingredients
When measuring liquids, use a clear glass or plastic measuring cup.
1. Place cup on a level surface.
2. Fill with liquid ingredient.
3. Check the measure at eye level.

How to peel a tomato
1. Using a sharp knife, remove stem end of tomato.
2. Cut a small cross in bottom of tomato.
3. Plunge tomato in a saucepan of boiling water for 20 seconds, then plunge in a bowl of ice water for 1 minute. Drain.
4. Starting from cross, peel off skin using a knife or fingertips.

How to seed a tomato
1. Cut round tomato in half crosswise, or plum (Roma) tomato in half lengthwise through stem.
2. If tomato is soft, squeeze with your hand to remove seeds. Or, if tomato is firm, use a teaspoon to scrape out seeds.

How to prepare fresh chili peppers

Fresh chili peppers range from mildly flavored to fiercely hot and are available year-round from supermarkets and greengrocers. Select firm chili peppers with smooth, glossy skin, dry stems and a fresh aroma. Store in a paper bag in the refrigerator, and use within 7 days. Generally, the smaller the chili the hotter!

1. Wear rubber gloves to avoid skin contact with capsaicin, the compound in chili peppers that carries the heat.
2. Using a sharp knife, cut as directed in recipe.
3. To lessen the intensity, cut in half lengthwise and remove seeds and membranes.

How to prepare an avocado

There are now many varieties of avocado available, from bright green to dark brown, though the skin does not generally indicate ripeness. When purchasing an avocado for use on the day, ask the greengrocer to help you, or very gently cradle the fruit in your hand to feel if it is supple to the touch. Hard unripe avocados should be left to ripen at room temperature, not in the refrigerator. Very hard fruit can take up to 5 days to ripen. To hasten ripening, place hard avocados in a brown paper bag with a ripe banana (the banana will emit ethylene gas, which accelerates ripening). Once ripe, use avocados within 1–2 days, or store in the refrigerator for 1–2 days before using.

Avocados turn brown quickly once cut, so it is best to prepare them just before serving. To delay discoloration, brush cut avocado flesh with fresh lemon juice.

1. Using a large sharp knife, cut avocado in half lengthwise all the way around the fruit, cutting around pit.
2. Gently twist halves in opposite directions to separate.
3. Lodge heel of knife into pit, and twist to remove.
4. To peel, place avocado half, flesh side down, on a cutting board. Starting at the narrow end, peel off skin using knife or fingertips.
5. Cut avocado flesh into slices, chop or mash, as directed by recipe.

How to prepare a bell pepper (capsicum)

1. If recipe calls for a whole bell pepper, use a sharp knife to cut off top crosswise, removing stem. Otherwise, cut bell pepper in half lengthwise through stem.
2. Using your fingers, remove seeds and white membrane from inside bell pepper and discard.
3. Place on cutting board and, using a sharp knife, cut as directed in recipe.

How to roast bell peppers (capsicums)

1. Grease a baking sheet; preheat oven to 425°F (220°C/Gas 7) or preheat a broiler (grill) to high heat.
2. Cut peppers in half lengthwise through stem. Remove seeds and membrane.
3. Place cut side down on baking sheet and bake or broil (grill) until skins are blistered and charred, about 15 minutes.
4. Transfer cooked bell peppers to a plastic bag, seal bag and let stand for 15 minutes.
5. Remove bell peppers from bag, then peel using fingers and discard skins.
6. To store, place roasted bell peppers in a jar and cover with extra virgin olive oil. Seal and store in refrigerator for up to 14 days. Use in salads, sandwiches and pasta sauces. (If oil solidifies in refrigerator, bring to room temperature before use.)

How to prepare fresh mushrooms

It is unnecessary to wash or peel fresh mushrooms.

1. Wipe mushrooms with a damp cloth to remove any dirt.
2. Using a sharp knife, trim stem end.

How to make a bouquet garni

A bouquet garni of herbs is added to stews, braises and soups during cooking to provide an aromatic flavor.

1. Prepare a clean piece of cheesecloth (muslin), about 5 in (13 cm) square.
2. Into center of cheesecloth, place 1 bay leaf, 1 sprig fresh thyme, a few sprigs fresh parsley and a few whole black peppercorns.
3. Gather edges of cheesecloth together, enclosing herbs, and tie in a bundle with kitchen string.
4. Use as directed in recipe, and remove and discard before serving.

How to make Parmesan cheese shavings

The younger the cheese, the better the shavings will be. Older cheeses are better tasting, but crumbly.

1. Using a vegetable peeler, remove thin slices from a wedge of Parmesan cheese.

How to remove kernels from an ear (cob) of corn

1. Strip husks and silk of corn down to stem end. Snap husks to remove, and pull away remaining silk.
2. Standing ear stem end down on cutting board, and using a sharp knife, cut downward, slicing close to cob, to remove kernels.

How to separate an egg

1. Gently but firmly crack a fresh egg on its equator against a hard surface, such as the edge of the countertop.
2. Over a clean bowl, carefully pull the eggshell halves apart. With an eggshell half in each hand, tip yolk from one half to the other, letting egg white slip into bowl underneath. Be careful not to break yolk.
3. Place egg yolk into a separate bowl.

HINT Check eggs for freshness (see page 30) before separating. Otherwise separate each egg before adding to other egg whites or egg yolks in recipe.

How to beat egg whites

Egg whites will beat to a greater volume if the eggs are at room temperature. Make sure you use a clean, grease-free bowl and utensils, and that there is no trace of yolk in the whites.

1. Place egg whites in a mixing bowl.
2. Using a balloon whisk or electric handheld or countertop mixer, beat until white and foamy: when whisk or mixer is lifted out of bowl, beaten egg white should stand up in "soft peaks" before slowly falling over.
3. Use immediately in recipe before egg whites lose their lightness.

How to whip cream

1. Place a medium-sized stainless steel or glass mixing bowl in the refrigerator to chill for 30 minutes.
2. Pour light (single) or double (heavy) cream into chilled bowl and beat using a balloon whisk or electric mixer until thick. Be careful not to overbeat the cream or it will separate.
3. Refrigerate to chill and use within 15 minutes.

How to melt chocolate

1. Place chopped chocolate in top of a double boiler, or in a heatproof bowl over simmering water in a small saucepan: do not let base of top saucepan or bowl touch water.
2. When chocolate begins to melt, stir with a wooden spoon until smooth and glossy.
3. Remove immediately from heat and use immediately in recipe.

How to bake blind

This is a cooking technique for prebaking a pie crust, without the filling, to ensure it stays crisp. It is commonly used for quiches, tarts and other pastries that contain a wet filling.

1. Preheat oven to 350°F (180°C/Gas 4).
2. Line baking pan with pie crust, as directed in recipe.
3. Cover pie crust with parchment (baking) paper, then fill with dried beans, rice or baking weights.
4. Bake for 15 minutes, then remove paper and beans, rice or weights.
5. Return pie crust, uncovered, to oven and bake until lightly golden, about 5 minutes.
6. Remove from oven and let cool at room temperature. The pie crust should be cooled completely before filling or using in recipe.

HINTS A prebaked pie crust may be stored in an airtight container for up to 5 days. Baking weights can be purchased at kitchenware stores. Rice and beans for baking blind may be reused for baking: simply store in an airtight jar or other container and make sure you label them.

How to warm plates

Warmed plates and bowls help to ensure that cooked foods, especially roast meats and pasta dishes, stay hot when they are served. They also add a luxurious touch to a homemade meal, but make sure you take appropriate care when handling them and that you warn guests if plates are hot.

1. Preheat oven to 300°F (150°C/Gas 2) and place serving plates or bowls (make sure they are heatproof) in oven for about 15 minutes before serving. Alternatively, place plates or bowls into a sink filled with hot water for 5 minutes, remove and dry thoroughly.
2. Use warmed plates or bowls immediately, as directed in recipe.

HINT Some ovens have a broiler (grill) attached directly above or below them, and, if the oven is already being used for cooking, it will conduct enough heat to warm your plates if they are placed there 30 minutes before serving. Some stove tops even have warming drawers.

Soups

There's nothing quite as comforting as homemade soup, whether you favor one of the classics or an invention of your own. Soups are convenient, nutritious and widely appealing. Best of all, anyone can make great soup.

Fundamental to a truly flavorsome homemade soup is the stock—it's always better to make your own. Homemade stock will give the soup a superior taste and add depth and richness to its flavor. However, if homemade stock is unavailable, you can use a good-quality stock from your supermarket instead. The best ready-made stocks do not contain added salt, preservatives or colorings.

With a good stock, making soup is easy. You can base the soup on what's in season, or use whatever is in your pantry, refrigerator or freezer, including leftovers. Be adventurous and substitute ingredients such as vegetables and herbs. Once you know the basics, the range of soups that you can make at home is infinite.

Purchasing soup ingredients
It's a great idea to buy soup ingredients such as vegetables and herbs in season. You are getting the produce at its peak, and it is also often more economical, as fruits and vegetables in their natural season tend to be cheaper. Stock up on soup basics such as onions, pumpkins or butternut squashes, celery, and herbs like parsley, which can be chopped and frozen.

Storing soups
Many soups keep well, either in the refrigerator or freezer (see recipes for specific keeping times). Once cooled, soup should be stored in an airtight container. For freezing, you can place the soup in individual portions in small sealed containers.

Soup cooking methods
For most soups, you will need a large saucepan with a tight-fitting lid. A blender or food processor is convenient for pureeing soups; alternatively, use a handheld (immersion) blender, or puree the soup by pushing it through a sieve with a wooden spoon.

Beef and vegetable soup

SERVES 6

INGREDIENTS

2 cobs (ears) of corn
2 tablespoons olive oil
1 lb (500 g) beef bones
1 lb (500 g) chuck steak, cubed
1 onion, chopped
10 cups (80 fl oz/2.5 L) water
2 bay leaves
5 whole black peppercorns
½ cup (3½ oz/100 g) pearl barley, rinsed and drained
2 carrots, peeled and chopped
2 celery stalks, chopped
2 medium potatoes, peeled and chopped
3 tomatoes, peeled, seeds removed and chopped (see page 17)
1 cup (5 oz/150 g) frozen green peas
2 tablespoons chopped fresh flat-leaf (Italian) parsley leaves

METHOD

1. Remove corn kernels from ears of corn (see page 19). Set aside.
2. In a large saucepan over medium heat, heat oil. Add bones and beef and cook, stirring, until browned, about 8 minutes.
3. Add onion, water, bay leaves and peppercorns, and stir. Bring to a boil, reduce heat to low, cover and simmer for 2 hours.
4. Remove and discard bones, and skim off any scum or fat from surface.
5. Add barley and stir, then cover and simmer a further 40 minutes.
6. Add carrots, celery, potatoes and tomatoes, and stir. Cover and simmer until vegetables are tender, about 20 minutes.
7. Add peas and corn kernels, and stir. Then cover and cook until tender, about 10 minutes.
8. Ladle into warmed serving bowls (see page 21), sprinkle with parsley and serve.

HINTS

- Pearl barley can be purchased from health food stores and some large supermarkets.
- Once cooled, soup may be stored in an airtight container in the refrigerator for up to 3 days.

Chicken and sweet corn soup

SERVES 4

INGREDIENTS
7 oz (220 g) skinless chicken breast fillet
1 teaspoon salt
2 egg whites
1 fresh ear (cob) of corn, husk and silk removed
6 cups (48 fl oz/1.5 L) Chicken Stock (see page 154)
1 tablespoon peeled and grated fresh ginger
1 can (14 oz/425 g) creamed corn
¼ cup (1 oz/30 g) cornstarch (cornflour)
⅓ cup (3 fl oz/90 ml) water
2 scallions (shallots/spring onions), finely chopped
½ teaspoon Asian sesame oil
1 teaspoon soy sauce

METHOD
1. Roughly chop chicken fillet, place in a food processor or blender and process until finely chopped. Transfer to a mixing bowl, add salt and stir.
2. In a small bowl, use a fork to beat egg whites until foamy. Fold egg whites into chicken.
3. Using a sharp knife, remove corn kernels from ear of corn (see page 19).
4. In a medium-sized saucepan over medium heat, bring stock to a boil. Reduce heat to low, add corn kernels, ginger and creamed corn, and stir. Simmer, uncovered, until corn is tender, about 5 minutes.
5. In a small bowl, stir cornstarch and water together until smooth. Add to soup, increase heat to medium and cook, stirring, until soup thickens, about 5 minutes.
6. Reduce heat to low and add chicken, stirring and breaking it up with a whisk, until chicken is cooked and changes color, about 3 minutes. Do not boil.
7. Add scallions, sesame oil and soy sauce. Cook, stirring, until heated through, about 2 minutes.
8. Ladle into serving bowls and serve immediately.

HINT Once cooled, soup may be stored in an airtight container in the refrigerator for up to 2 days.

Chicken noodle soup

Once you've had real homemade chicken noodle soup, the instant variety will never taste as good. Here's my version of this family favorite.

SERVES 4

INGREDIENTS
1 lb (500 g) chicken thighs (with bone)
1 yellow (brown) onion, chopped
1 leek, sliced
2 celery stalks, chopped
2 carrots, peeled and chopped
3 whole black peppercorns
2 bay leaves
2 sprigs fresh parsley
12 cups (96 fl oz/3 L) water
4 oz (125 g) thin vermicelli spaghetti
sea salt and freshly ground black pepper
2 tablespoons chopped fresh parsley leaves

METHOD
1. In a large saucepan over medium heat, combine chicken, onion, leek, celery, carrot, peppercorns, bay leaves, parsley sprigs and water.
2. Bring to a boil and, using a slotted spoon, remove any scum from surface.
3. Reduce heat to low and simmer, uncovered, for 2 hours.
4. Remove chicken from soup and set aside to cool. Remove and discard skin and bone from chicken, then chop flesh into ½-in (12-mm) cubes.
5. Add chopped chicken to soup and bring to a boil over high heat.
6. Break spaghetti into 2-in (5-cm) pieces, then add to soup. Reduce heat to medium and cook until spaghetti is tender, about 10 minutes.
7. Season soup with salt and pepper to taste. Ladle into warm serving bowls, sprinkle with chopped parsley, and serve immediately.

HINT Once cooled, soup may be stored in an airtight container in the refrigerator for up to 2 days.

VARIATION Chinese Chicken Noodle Soup
Use thin Chinese egg noodles in place of spaghetti, season to taste with soy sauce instead of salt, and use chopped scallions (shallots/spring onions) instead of parsley.

French onion soup

SERVES 4

INGREDIENTS
2 oz (60 g) butter
5 yellow (brown) onions, sliced
2 cloves garlic, crushed (see page 16) (see page 16)
2 tablespoons all-purpose (plain) flour
8 cups (64 fl oz/2 L) Beef Stock (see page 153)
sea salt and freshly ground black pepper
8 thick slices French bread
⅓ cup (45 g/1½ oz) grated Swiss cheese
2 tablespoons chopped fresh parsley leaves

METHOD
1. In a large saucepan over medium heat, melt butter. Add onion and garlic, reduce heat to low and cook, stirring, until golden, about 20 minutes.
2. Add flour and cook, stirring, until golden, about 1 minute.
3. Remove pan from heat and gradually add stock, stirring constantly. Season with salt and pepper.
4. Return saucepan to high heat and bring to a boil. Reduce heat to low, cover and simmer for 30 minutes.
5. Preheat broiler (grill) to high heat. Place bread slices on a broiler (grill) rack and broil (grill) until lightly golden on one side. Turn bread over and top each slice with grated cheese. Broil (grill) until cheese melts and bread is golden.
6. Place 2 slices cheese toast into each serving bowl. Ladle hot soup over toast, sprinkle with parsley, and serve immediately.

HINT Once cooled, soup may be stored in an airtight container in the refrigerator for 1–2 days; however, the onion flavor will be much stronger after storing.

Garden vegetable soup

SERVES 4

INGREDIENTS
2 tablespoons olive oil
1 onion, chopped
2 zucchini (courgettes), chopped
2 celery stalks, chopped
4 oz (125 g) button mushrooms, sliced
2 carrots, peeled and sliced
1 medium potato, peeled and chopped
1 lb (500 g) pumpkin or butternut squash, peeled and chopped
¾ cup (5 oz/150 g) brown lentils, rinsed and drained
8 cups (64 fl oz/2 L) Vegetable Stock (see page 155)
sea salt and freshly ground black pepper
crusty bread, for serving

METHOD
1. In a large saucepan over medium heat, heat oil. Add onion and cook, stirring, until onion softens, about 1 minute.
2. Add zucchini, celery and mushrooms, and cook, stirring, until vegetables soften, about 4 minutes.
3. Add carrot, potato, pumpkin or squash, lentils and stock, and stir. Bring to a boil, then reduce heat to low, cover and cook until lentils and vegetables are soft, 30–35 minutes.
4. Season to taste with salt and pepper. Ladle into warmed soup bowls (see page 21), and serve with crusty bread.

HINTS
• If soup is too thick, add extra vegetable stock to taste.
• Once cooled, soup may be stored in an airtight container in the refrigerator for up to 5 days.

VARIATION Cream of Vegetable Soup
Working in batches, ladle finished soup into a food processor or blender and process until smooth, then return to saucepan. Add ½ cup (4 fl oz/125 ml) light (single) cream and gently heat through. Do not let boil. (If soup is too thick, add extra stock.)

Minestrone

This hearty Italian soup is a meal in itself; serve with crusty bread and a good red wine. You can use any type of small pasta, such as tiny penne or shells, and you can substitute red kidney beans for the cannellini beans.

SERVES 4

INGREDIENTS
2 tablespoons olive oil
2 onions, chopped
2 cloves garlic, crushed (see page 16)
4 slices thick-cut bacon, rind removed and roughly chopped
1 carrot, peeled and chopped
1 can (14 oz/425 g) crushed tomatoes
8 cups (64 fl oz/2 L) Beef Stock (see page 153)
1 medium potato, peeled and chopped
1 celery stalk, chopped
2 tablespoons tomato paste
1 cup (3 oz/90 g) shredded cabbage
½ cup (2½ oz/75 g) fresh or frozen green peas
½ cup (2 oz/60 g) small macaroni
1½ cups (10 oz/300 g) canned cannellini beans, rinsed and drained
sea salt and freshly ground black pepper
2 tablespoons chopped fresh flat-leaf (Italian) parsley leaves
⅓ cup (1½ oz/45 g) Parmesan cheese shavings

METHOD
1. In a large saucepan over medium heat, heat oil. Add onions, garlic, bacon and carrot, and cook, stirring, until bacon browns, about 4 minutes.
2. Add tomatoes and stock, and stir. Bring to a boil, reduce heat to low, cover and simmer for 25 minutes.
3. Add potato, celery and tomato paste, and stir. Cover and simmer until potato is tender, about 15 minutes.
4. Add cabbage, peas, macaroni and cannellini beans, and stir. Cover and simmer until pasta is tender, about 10 minutes.
5. Season to taste with salt and pepper. Ladle into warmed serving bowls (see page 21), and sprinkle with parsley and Parmesan cheese.

HINT Soup may be stored in an airtight container in the refrigerator for up to 4 days; it will thicken, so add beef stock when reheating if required.

Pumpkin soup

SERVES 4

INGREDIENTS
2 lb (1 kg) pumpkin or butternut squash
2 tablespoons butter
1 yellow (brown) onion, chopped
2 slices thick-cut bacon, rind removed and chopped
4 cups (32 fl oz/1 L) Chicken Stock (see page 154)
¼ cup (2 fl oz/60 ml) light (single) cream
sea salt and freshly ground black pepper
2 tablespoons chopped fresh parsley leaves
4 fresh crusty bread rolls or warm buttered toast, for serving

METHOD
1. Using a sharp knife, remove skin and seeds from pumpkin or squash. Cut into rough chunks about 2 in (5 cm) in size.
2. In a large saucepan over medium heat, melt butter. Add onion and bacon, and cook, stirring, until onion softens, about 1–2 minutes.
3. Add pumpkin pieces and stock, and stir. Bring to a boil, reduce heat to medium–low, then cover and simmer until pumpkin has softened, about 25 minutes.
4. Remove saucepan from heat. Working in batches, carefully ladle soup into a food processor or blender and process to a thick puree.
5. Return soup to saucepan, and add cream and salt and pepper to taste. Stir over low heat until heated through. Do not allow to boil.
6. Ladle soup into warmed serving bowls (see page 21) and sprinkle with chopped parsley. Serve immediately with fresh crusty bread rolls or warm buttered toast.

HINTS
- Do not let soup boil once you have added cream or it may curdle.
- Choose firm bright pumpkins or butternut squashes with no soft spots or cracks. Store whole in a cool dry place. Cut pieces should be moist, with no signs of soft spots. Remove seeds from cut pumpkin, and store it wrapped in plastic wrap in the crisper section of the refrigerator for up to 5 days.
- Once cooled, soup may be stored in an airtight container in the refrigerator for up to 4 days. When reheating, do not allow soup to boil or it may curdle.

Eggs

The humble egg is one of my favorite foods. Where would we be without it? Eggs can be boiled, fried, poached, baked, flipped, whipped and folded into so many things, fancy or simple. They are full of goodness and flavor, and conveniently packaged too!

With eggs in the pantry or refrigerator, you'll always have ingredients for a meal, but do make sure you buy the freshest quality available. If possible, choose eggs labeled organic and/or free-range or cage-free eggs that are available at most supermarkets, and you'll discover what an egg should taste like! The difference in flavor between these eggs and commercially farmed eggs is vast. Organic eggs tend to have richly-colored, deep yellow yolks, which is just a reflection of the diet the laying chicken has enjoyed.

This chapter contains the basics of cooking eggs—from how to boil an egg or make great scrambled eggs to French toast, quiche and frittata. There are recipes that suit breakfast, brunch, lunch, and dinner, such is the versatility of an egg in the kitchen.

Purchasing eggs
Eggs are sold by size, usually the larger the egg the greater the amount of egg white. The large egg (size 5), which weighs 2 oz (60 g), is the most commonly used egg in cookery. There is no nutritional difference between eggs with brown or white shells. Chicken eggs are the standard, but duck, goose, and quail eggs are also available. Always check the use-by date on the egg carton.

Storing eggs
Eggs should always be stored with the pointed end down in their carton in the refrigerator.

How to test if an egg is fresh
To test if an egg is fresh, place the whole egg in its shell carefully into a large bowl of cold water. If the egg sinks, it's fresh. If the egg floats, it's old and should not be used.

Egg cooking methods

How to boil eggs

Boiled eggs are an all-time favorite—whether soft for breakfast with fingers of hot buttered toast or hard, cooled, sliced and added to sandwiches or salads. For a special brunch or starter, serve soft-boiled eggs with steamed fresh asparagus: dip asparagus into runny yolk and enjoy with sea salt and plenty of freshly ground black pepper.

To prevent eggs from cracking during boiling, use fresh eggs at room temperature or remove eggs from refrigerator 1–2 hours before cooking.

1. Choose a saucepan to hold the number of eggs required. Place eggs in a single layer in saucepan, then cover with cold water.
2. Place saucepan over medium heat and bring to a boil.
3. Boil, uncovered, for 4 minutes for a soft yolk; and 5 minutes for a hard-boiled yolk.
4. Remove egg from saucepan using a slotted spoon and serve in an eggcup.

HINT If using hard-boiled eggs cold in salads or sandwiches, drain boiling water after cooking, then refill saucepan with cold water. After about 1 minute, peel eggs and place in a clean bowl of cold water until cold, about 5 minutes. This will prevent a gray ring from forming around egg yolk.

How to fry eggs

For perfectly formed fried eggs, use an egg ring, available in sets from most kitchenware shops or some large supermarkets. Otherwise, the fried egg will simply form it's own unique shape—which some people prefer!

1 In a nonstick frying pan over medium heat, heat enough oil (olive or vegetable) to just cover base of pan.
2. Oil egg rings, if using, and place in pan. Break eggs into egg rings or directly in pan.
3. For "sunny-side up" eggs, cook for about 2 minutes, spooning a little of the oil in pan over eggs to help them cook. For "easy over" eggs, flip eggs using a spatula (egg slide) and cook to your taste, about a further 1 minute.
4. Remove from pan, then remove eggs rings if using. Serve on hot buttered toast.

HINT Serve fried eggs with crispy-fried bacon slices and broiled (grilled) tomato halves.

How to poach eggs

Poached eggs are delicious and healthy. Serve on hot buttered toast, cooled in sandwiches or with salads, or with barbecued steaks.

1. Grease or oil egg rings.
2. Fill a frying pan with ½ in (12 mm) water, and add 1 teaspoon white vinegar and pinch salt. Bring to a boil over high heat then reduce heat to low, so water is barely simmering.
3. Place egg rings in water. Break an egg into a cup, then gently pour egg into a ring.
4. As egg cooks (the egg white starts cooking first), spoon a little of the hot water from pan over yolk. Cook egg to your liking.
5. Carefully remove egg ring from egg while in water, then remove egg from pan using a slotted spoon. Drain on a clean kitchen towel or paper towels before serving immediately.

HINT Use the freshest eggs for poaching, as the white of an older egg will be watery and will not hold its shape during cooking.

How to scramble eggs

The secret to great scrambled eggs is a good heavy-based saucepan or frying pan and a little patience. Quickly cooked scrambled eggs will be tough! Once cooked, you can add flavorings of choice, like grated cheese, chopped smoked salmon, shredded spinach or crispy pieces of broiled (grilled) bacon or prosciutto. Plan on 2 eggs per person.

1. Break 2 eggs into a mixing bowl, and add sea salt, freshly ground black pepper and freshly chopped herbs to taste. Add 1 tablespoon milk or light (single) cream and beat with a fork until combined.
2. In a frying pan or saucepan over medium heat, melt about 1 tablespoon butter. Reduce heat to low and add egg mixture.
3. As mixture starts to set on base of pan, gently fold cooked edges over using a wooden spoon. Continue cooking, folding over edges of egg, until slightly firm but still creamy.
4. Spoon onto a thick slice of warm buttered toast to serve.

HINT Do not vigorously stir eggs while cooking or your scrambled eggs will be crumbly and watery.

Fluffy omelet with cheese and spinach

SERVES 1–2

INGREDIENTS
3 eggs
2 tablespoons butter
3 tablespoons grated tasty cheese
1 tablespoon chopped fresh chives
sea salt and freshly ground black pepper to taste
6 baby spinach leaves, rinsed

METHOD
1. Separate eggs (see page 20). In a mixing bowl, stir egg yolks together using a fork.
2. Place egg whites in a separate bowl and using a whisk or electric mixer, beat until soft peaks form.
3. Fold egg whites into egg yolks.
4. Heat a flameproof 10-in (25-cm) nonstick frying pan over medium heat and add butter. When butter sizzles, pour in egg mixture evenly over base of pan. Reduce heat to low and cook until set and golden brown underneath, about 5 minutes.
5. Preheat broiler (grill) to high temperature. Remove pan from heat and sprinkle top of omelet with cheese, chives and salt and pepper. Place omelet in frying pan under broiler (grill) and cook until cheese melts, 1–2 minutes.
6. Remove frying pan from broiler (grill) and sprinkle spinach leaves over cheese.
7. Gently fold omelet in half, so that spinach and cheese is enclosed in center, while sliding it from pan onto a serving plate. Let stand for 2–3 minutes before serving.

HINTS
- Eggs should be at room temperature for best results; remove them from the refrigerator 30 minutes before using.
- Make sure you use a clean bowl when beating the egg whites.

French toast

SERVES 4

INGREDIENTS
4 eggs
½ cup (4 fl oz/125 ml) milk
2 tablespoons superfine (caster) sugar
¼ teaspoon vanilla extract (essence)
2 tablespoons butter
8 thick slices white bread
maple syrup, for serving

METHOD
1. In a large bowl, combine eggs, milk, sugar and vanilla. Mix together using a fork or whisk.
2. In a medium-sized frying pan over medium heat, melt butter.
3. Meanwhile, working in batches, dip bread slices one at a time into egg mixture; bread should be completely coated and should soak up some of mixture.
4. Place bread into frying pan in a single layer and cook until golden underneath, about 1 minute. Then turn slices over and cook other side for a further 1 minute. Remove from pan and set aside on a plate lined with paper towels. Repeat with remaining bread.
5. Transfer to serving plates and drizzle with maple syrup to taste. Serve immediately.

Quiche Lorraine

The pie crust for this recipe is made in the food processor, which makes it very quick and easy. So even if you've never made pie crust before, you can be successful with this simple method. Overhandling, however, will make the pie crust tough and dry, so make sure you don't overwork it, either when rolling or in the food processor.

SERVES 6

INGREDIENTS

For pie crust
1⅔ cups (8 oz/250 g) all-purpose (plain) flour
3½ oz (100 g) butter, chopped
pinch salt
2 tablespoons chilled water

For filling
4 slices thick-cut bacon, rind removed and chopped
1 cup (4 oz/125 g) grated Gruyère or tasty cheese
2 whole eggs
2 egg yolks
1 cup (8 fl oz/250 ml) light (single) cream
sea salt and freshly ground black pepper to taste

METHOD

1. To make pie crust: Place flour, butter and salt in a food processor. Process until mixture resembles fine bread crumbs, about 1 minute. Add water and pulse until mixture comes together, about 20 seconds.
2. Shape dough into disc, wrap in plastic wrap, and refrigerate for 30 minutes.
3. Using a rolling pin, roll out pie crust between two sheets of floured parchment (baking) paper into a round circle 12 in (30 cm) in diameter. Line a 9-in (23-cm) pan with pie crust; it should cover base and sides and slightly overhang the rim. Refrigerate for a further 30 minutes. Place pie pan on a baking sheet.
4. Preheat oven to 350°F (180°C/Gas 4). Blind bake pie crust (see page 19).
5. To make filling: In a nonstick frying pan over medium heat, fry bacon until golden and crisp, about 4 minutes. Remove from pan using a slotted spoon and drain on paper towels until cool.

6. Spread bacon and cheese evenly over base of cooled pie crust.
7. In a pitcher or mixing bowl, combine whole eggs, egg yolks, cream and season with salt and pepper. Using a whisk or fork, blend together. Pour evenly over bacon and cheese.
8. Bake until golden and filling is set, 25–30 minutes. Serve warm with Green Salad (see page 86).

HINT You can make the pie crust in advance. After baking blind, store cooled crust in an airtight container in the refrigerator for up to 5 days. The unbaked pie crusts may also be stored in the freezer.

Roast-vegetable frittata

If you have leftover roast vegetables (I never seem to!), you can use them for this recipe. Serve warm with Green Salad (see page 86) and crusty bread.

SERVES 4

INGREDIENTS

1 lb (500 g) sweet potatoes or yams (kumara), peeled and chopped
1 red bell pepper (capsicum), seeds removed and cut into 8 wedges (see page 18)
2 zucchini (courgettes), chopped
2 medium potatoes, peeled and chopped
2 red onions, cut into 8 wedges
3 tablespoons olive oil
1 teaspoon sea salt
6 eggs
1 cup (8 fl oz/250 ml) light (single) cream
¼ cup (1 oz/30 g) grated tasty cheese
¼ cup (1 oz/30 g) grated Parmesan cheese
freshly ground black pepper
1 tablespoon chopped fresh flat-leaf (Italian) parsley leaves
1 tablespoon torn or shredded fresh basil leaves

METHOD

1. Preheat oven to 350°F (180°C/Gas 4). Line a large baking pan with parchment (baking) paper. Place sweet potatoes, bell pepper, zucchini, potato and onion in a single layer in pan.
2. Drizzle vegetables with olive oil, sprinkle with sea salt and bake until golden, about 30 minutes.
3. Remove from oven and transfer vegetables to a deep, flameproof 9-in (23-cm) nonstick frying pan. Arrange vegetables evenly over base of pan.
4. In a medium-sized bowl, combine eggs, cream, tasty and Parmesan cheeses, pepper and parsley. Whisk until well combined.
5. Pour egg mixture evenly over vegetables in pan and sprinkle with basil. Place pan over low heat and cook, without stirring, until egg mixture sets, about 10 minutes.
6. Meanwhile, preheat broiler (grill) to high heat. Broil (grill) frittata until top is golden, about 2 minutes. Let stand in pan for 5 minutes. Cut into wedges to serve.

Meat

I'm always surprised at how many people are afraid to cook meat—and not just the vegetarians! Beginners often think of meat as "too difficult," while others complain that it's "fussy." But these days, the quality and variety of meat available in supermarkets, butchers and delicatessens make cooking with meat easy.

Finding a good meat supplier will halve your cooking effort! Not only will you be assured of quality, but also of a wide selection of cuts. The best meat suppliers will offer friendly advice, and will also cut, chop or debone the meat as required, saving you time—what could be easier!

This chapter includes traditional family favorites, such as roasted leg of lamb, with mint sauce of course, hamburgers and cottage pie. You'll also find some of the new classics like steak sandwich, Thai beef salad, and beef and noodle stir-fry. Don't forget, however, that good meat is often best when simply cooked, whether broiled (grilled), barbecued or quickly panfried.

Purchasing meat

When choosing meat, consider its cost versus the time required to cook it. Tender cuts are the most expensive, but are quick to cook and will save you time. Less tender cuts are a lot cheaper, but require more time for preparation and cooking to ensure good results.

A good meat supplier will gladly do the preparation—if required, ask the butcher to cut or debone the meat for you. He or she has the skill, and the sharpest knives, to remove bones without too much waste, slice steak for stir-frying, or chop meat for casseroles.

Make sure you get your meat purchases home quickly to the refrigerator, and if shopping on hot days, use an insulated cooler (eski) to keep meat cool.

When purchasing meat, look for the following signs of freshness:
- Beef—flesh should be a good red color, connective fibers should be small with a slight marbling of fat. Fat should be cream colored and have a fresh smell.
- Lamb—flesh should be pinkish red and finely grained. Any bones should be small.
- Pork—flesh should be a pale pink and finely grained with very little connective tissue. Fat should be smooth, white and oily.
- Veal—flesh should be soft and pink.

Storing meat

Fresh meat is highly perishable and should be stored in the coldest part of your refrigerator. As soon as possible after purchase, remove meat from its tray or plastic bag. Line a plate with paper towels and place meat in a single layer on top, then loosely cover with plastic wrap. Do not stack cuts of meat on top of one another. Keep for up to 3–4 days in the refrigerator.

To freeze fresh meat, place in a plastic freezer bag or airtight container. Make sure it is well-sealed to prevent meat from drying out or discoloring, and to stop the formation of ice crystals. Label and date to ensure meat is eaten within its optimum recommended freezing time.

Freezing guide

Cuts of beef, lamb, pork and veal—6 months
Ground (minced) meat—4 months
Sausages—3 months

Meat cooking methods

How to barbecue, pan grill, broil (grill)

These quick cooking methods require tender cuts of meat: beef sirloin (rump), T-bone, rib-eye (scotch fillet), tenderloin (fillet) or porterhouse (sirloin) steaks, or marinated round or blade steak; lamb tenderloin (fillet), cutlets or back straps, or marinated loin chops; and pork tenderloin, fillet or butterfly steaks, or marinated leg steaks.

1. Preheat barbecue, grill pan or broiler (grill) until hot. Do not oil cooking plate, as this causes lots of smoke!
2. Season meat with freshly ground black pepper and herbs, if desired, and brush with olive oil. If broiling (grilling), place on broiler (grill) rack.
3. Place meat on barbecue or grill pan, or place broiler rack under broiler, and cook until meat changes color, about 2 minutes. Turn with tongs and cook on other side, a further 2 minutes for rare and remove from pan.
4. Or reduce heat and continue to cook until done to your liking, about 1–2 minutes for medium or 3–4 minutes for well-done.

HINT Instead of brushing with olive oil, marinate meat (see page 156) before cooking to increase flavor and tenderness.

How to make a casserole or stew

These are slow, moist cooking methods that are ideal for cheaper, tougher cuts, such as beef chuck, lamb shoulder or shank, and pork shoulder, that become tender with the long cooking time. This style of cooking is especially popular in the colder seasons.

1. In a large heavy-based saucepan or flameproof baking dish (casserole) over medium heat, heat oil.
2. Add ingredients as directed in recipe; for example, onion and meat, then stock or sauces, vegetables, spices and herbs.
3. Cover pan or baking dish. Cook over very low heat or in a preheated oven, as directed in recipe, until meat is tender, 1–2 hours.

How to panfry

This quick method of cooking requires a tender cut of meat. For example, beef sirloin (rump), tenderloin, fillet or porterhouse; lamb tenderloin, fillet, cutlets, boneless leg steaks or loin chops; and pork tenderloin, loin chops, fillet, butterfly steaks, schnitzel and medallion.

1. Heat a heavy-based frying pan over medium heat until hot, 3–4 minutes.
2. Brush meat lightly with olive oil and sprinkle with freshly ground black pepper.
3. Using tongs, place meat in pan. Cook until juices rise to uncooked side, 1–2 minutes. Then turn meat over and cook until done to your liking, a further 1 minute for medium–rare, or 2 minutes for medium to well-done.

HINT Instead of brushing with olive oil, marinate meat (see page 156) before cooking to increase flavor and tenderness.

How to stir-fry

This very quick method of cooking requires tender cuts of meat, cut into similar-sized pieces to ensure even cooking. Suitable cuts include beef sirloin (rump), beef round (topside); lamb tenderloin (fillet) or loin (back straps); and pork tenderloin (fillet) or leg steak. Meat may be marinated (see page 156) before stir-frying.

1. Heat a wok or deep nonstick frying pan over high heat until very hot, then add oil.
2. Drain meat from marinade, if using, and working in batches, add meat to wok or pan and cook, stirring and tossing with a wooden spoon or spatula, until meat changes color, 3–5 minutes. Remove from wok and set aside. Repeat until all meat is cooked.
3. Stir-fry other ingredients as directed in recipe, then return meat to pan (this prevents meat from stewing and overcooking).
4. Add flavorings like oyster and soy sauces at the end of cooking. Serve immediately for best flavor and texture.

HINT A wok is best for stir-frying, as the sloping sides make it easy to toss and turn food during cooking. If unavailable, use a deep nonstick frying pan. Make sure the wok or pan is very hot before anything is added.

How to roast

This is a long, dry cooking method which suits both tender and tough cuts. Tougher or larger cuts of meat such as beef round (topside), leg of lamb and pork shoulder will require slower cooking at a lower temperature. Tender cuts suitable for roasting include whole rib-eye (scotch fillet), rack of lamb and pork fillet, and these require a higher oven temperature and shorter cooking time for optimum results.

1. Preheat oven as directed in recipe.
2. Brush meat with olive oil and season, then place in a baking pan along with any other ingredients.
3. Bake, uncovered, until tender, then let rest before serving.

How to rest a roast

The most important step to a successful roast is to allow the meat to rest once it is cooked. "Resting" ensures juices are retained to keep meat moist and tender.

1. Transfer cooked roast immediately from baking pan to a warm platter.
2. Cover with aluminum foil and let stand for 20 minutes before carving.

How to serve a hot roast dinner

Both new and experienced cooks often say to me that serving a hot roast dinner is stressful! They struggle to ensure that everything hits the table at the same time—meat, vegetables, gravy and anything else on the side, let alone the diners.

The secret to preventing a roast dinner from going cold while serving is to warm the dinner plates (see above). Then follow these simple steps, and your roast will be served hot every time.

1. Once roasted meat and vegetables are ready, transfer meat from baking pan to a platter for resting (see above). Transfer vegetables from pan to warmed dinner plates and return to oven at 225°F (110°C/Gas ¼) to keep warm.
2. Make gravy in baking pan while meat is resting.
3. When ready to serve, carve meat and place straight onto warm dinner plates, next to cooked vegetables. Spoon hot gravy over top.
4. If required, return all plated meals to warm oven until diners are ready. (This is a trick my mother used to keep the food hot until all of her four children were quietly seated at the table.) Remember to warn your guests that plates are hot to the touch!

Basic roast beef

Ask your butcher to prepare a standing rib roast (joint) for oven roasting, so that you will be able to slice through the ribs easily when carving to serve.

SERVES 6

INGREDIENTS
4 lb (2 kg) standing rib roast (joint)
olive oil
sea salt and freshly ground black pepper

METHOD
1. Preheat oven to 450°F (230°C/Gas 8). Place beef in a roasting pan, cover with a clean kitchen towel or plastic wrap, and let stand at room temperature for 20 minutes.
2. Using a basting (glazing) brush, brush beef with olive oil, then season with sea salt and freshly ground black pepper.
3. Bake for 20 minutes, then reduce oven temperature to 350°F (180°C/ Gas 4) and bake until cooked to your taste, a further 1 hour to 1 hour and 20 minutes (see Beef Roasting Time Guide below).
4. Remove beef from oven, transfer from pan to a warm platter, cover with aluminum foil and let rest for 20 minutes (see page 41).
5. Carve beef and serve with Crispy Roast Potatoes (see page 126) and Roast Meat Gravy (see opposite).

BEEF ROASTING TIME GUIDE
Allow 20 minutes per 1 lb (500 g) beef roast (on the bone) for medium-rare.
Allow 25 minutes per 1 lb (500 g) for well-done.

Roast meat gravy

The taste of homemade gravy is well worth the little effort it takes. Using the pan juices from the roast, gravy can be made easily while the cooked meat is resting. For best results, use homemade stock, but if unavailable substitute a good quality ready-made version from the supermarket.

SERVES 4

INGREDIENTS
pan juices from roast meat
3 tablespoons all-purpose (plain) flour
½ cup (4 fl oz/125 ml) red wine
2 cups (16 fl oz/500 ml) Beef Stock (see page 153)
sea salt and freshly ground black pepper

METHOD
1. While roast meat is resting (see page 41), pour off pan juices from roasting pan, reserving about ½ cup (4 fl oz/125 ml) for gravy.
2. Place roasting pan, with reserved pan juices, over medium heat. Sprinkle flour over juices and cook, stirring constantly, until flour is lightly golden, 1–2 minutes.
3. Remove pan from heat and gradually blend in wine and stock.
4. Return pan to medium heat and cook, stirring, until gravy thickens. Season with sea salt and pepper to taste, adding a little more stock if gravy is too thick.

HINTS
• When seasoning, add your choice of chopped fresh herbs or sprinkle of dried herbs to taste.
• For added flavor, broil (grill) the flour before using it to make gravy. To do this, preheat a broiler (grill) to high heat. Sprinkle flour evenly on a baking sheet then broil (grill) until golden. You can make extra quantities of gravy flour, let it cool, then store in an airtight container.

Basic roast lamb with potatoes

This traditional roast uses a leg of lamb, but you could ask your butcher to bone, roll and tie it with string if you prefer. A boned, rolled leg is easy to carve, and takes less cooking time. For example, a 3-lb (1.5-kg) leg of lamb, boned, needs to cook for only about 45 minutes.

SERVES 4–6

INGREDIENTS
3 lb (1.5 kg) leg of lamb
olive oil
sea salt and freshly ground black pepper
1 handful fresh rosemary sprigs
8 medium potatoes, peeled and halved

METHOD
1. Preheat oven to 400°F (200°C/Gas 6). Place leg of lamb in a roasting pan, cover and let stand at room temperature for 20 minutes.
2. Transfer lamb from roasting pan to a large plate. Using a basting (glazing) brush, brush lamb with olive oil, then season with sea salt and freshly ground black pepper.
3. Scatter rosemary sprigs over base of roasting pan. Place lamb on top of rosemary. Arrange potatoes around lamb. Brush potatoes with olive oil
4. Roast for 20 minutes. Remove pan from oven, baste lamb with pan juices and turn potatoes. Return to oven and roast lamb until cooked to your taste, a further 25–40 minutes (see Lamb Roasting Time Guide below), turning potatoes twice more.
5. When lamb is cooked, transfer to a warmed platter, cover with aluminum foil and let rest for 20 minutes (see page 41). Return potatoes to oven and roast until golden and crisp, about 10 minutes.
6. Carve lamb and serve with roasted potatoes and Mint Sauce (see opposite).

LAMB ROASTING TIME GUIDE
Allow 15 minutes per 1 lb (500 g) for roast lamb with a pink center.
Allow 20 minutes per 1 lb (500 g) for well-done lamb.

Mint sauce

INGREDIENTS
3 tablespoons finely chopped fresh mint leaves
1 tablespoon white sugar
3 tablespoons boiling water
3 tablespoons malt or cider vinegar

METHOD
1. Place mint in a small heatproof bowl. Add sugar and boiling water, and stir until sugar dissolves.
2. Add vinegar and stir. Let stand for 1 hour at room temperature before serving with roast lamb.

Applesauce for basic roast pork

SERVES 4

INGREDIENTS
3 green cooking apples
2 tablespoons water
2 tablespoons white sugar
1-in (2.5-cm) piece lemon peel

METHOD
1. Peel, core and roughly chop apples.
2. Place apples in a small saucepan, add water, sugar and peel, and stir. Cook, covered, over low heat until soft and pulpy, 4–5 minutes, adding more water if needed.
3. Remove pan from heat and discard peel. Serve sauce warm or cold, with Basic Roast Pork (page 46).

HINT Applesauce can be made in advance, and stored in an airtight container for 1–2 days in the refrigerator. To reheat, place in a small saucepan and stir over low heat until heated through.

Basic roast pork

Ask your butcher to score the rind of pork, as this will make it easier to break into pieces to serve.

SERVES 4–6

INGREDIENTS
3 lb (1.5 kg) pork shoulder with rind intact, rind scored
salt
freshly ground black pepper

METHOD
1. Preheat oven to 400°F (200°C/Gas 6). Pat pork dry with paper towels then rub salt into pork rind. Place pork in a roasting pan, cover and let stand at room temperature for 20 minutes.
2. Bake pork for 20 minutes, reduce oven temperature to 350°F (180°C/ Gas 4) and roast until juices run clear when thickest part of pork is pierced with a skewer, a further 1 hour and 10 minutes.
3. Remove pork from oven, then remove rind from meat to make crackling.
4. Place meat on a warm platter, cover with aluminum foil and rest for 20 minutes (see page 41).
5. Return pork rind to oven and roast until crisp, about 10 minutes. Remove from oven and let cool, then break into serving pieces.
6. Carve meat and serve with pieces of crackling, Crispy Roast Potatoes (see page 126) and Applesauce (see page 45).

PORK ROASTING TIME GUIDE
Allow 30 minutes per 1 lb (500 g) of pork.

Beef casserole

SERVES 4–6

INGREDIENTS
½ cup (2½ oz/75 g) all-purpose (plain) flour
sea salt and freshly ground black pepper
3 lb (1.5 kg) boneless beef chuck (blade) steak, cut into large cubes
3 tablespoons olive oil
3 medium potatoes, cut into chunks
2 onions, chopped
1 clove garlic, crushed (see page 16)
2 carrots, peeled and cut into chunks
1 can (14 oz/425 g) crushed tomatoes
½ cup (4 fl oz/125 ml) red wine
1 cup (8 fl oz/250 ml) Beef Stock (see page 153)
steamed rice (see page 110) and crusty bread, for serving

METHOD
1. Preheat oven to 350°F (180°C/Gas 4). Grease an 8-cup (64-fl oz/2-L) baking dish with lid.
2. Place flour in a plastic bag and season with salt and pepper. Add beef pieces, tossing until coated in flour. Remove beef from bag and shake off excess flour.
3. In a medium-sized frying pan over medium heat, heat olive oil. Working in batches, add beef and cook until brown on all sides, 4–5 minutes. Remove from pan using a slotted spoon and drain on paper towels. Repeat until all meat is cooked. Place meat and potatoes into baking dish.
4. Add onions, garlic and carrots to frying pan and cook, stirring, until vegetables are lightly golden. Stir in tomatoes, wine and stock. Bring to a boil, reduce heat to medium and cook for 5 minutes.
5. Pour vegetables and sauce over meat and potatoes in baking dish, and mix to coat with sauce. Cover and bake until meat is tender, about 1½ hours.
6. Season with sea salt and pepper to taste. Serve with steamed rice and crusty bread.

Beef and noodle stir-fry

SERVES 4

INGREDIENTS
5 oz (150 g) rice stick noodles
2 tablespoons soy sauce
3 tablespoons hoisin sauce
2 cloves garlic, crushed (see page 16)
2 teaspoons peeled and grated fresh ginger
12 oz (375 g) round (topside) or sirloin (rump) steak, thinly sliced
2 tablespoons vegetable oil
6 button mushrooms, sliced
2 tablespoons Beef Stock (see page 157)
1 tablespoon dry sherry
1 teaspoon Asian sesame oil

METHOD
1. Cook noodles as directed on package (or see page 107). Drain and set aside.
2. In a glass or ceramic bowl, combine soy and hoisin sauces, garlic and ginger. Add steak slices and turn to coat in marinade. Cover and marinate for 30 minutes. Drain steak and reserve marinade.
3. In a wok or frying pan over medium heat, heat vegetable oil. Add steak and stir-fry until meat changes color, 3–4 minutes. Remove meat from pan and set aside.
4. Return pan to medium–high heat, add mushrooms, scallions and broccoli, and stir-fry for 2 minutes. Add noodles, steak, reserved marinade, beef stock, sherry and sesame oil, and stir-fry until heated through, 2–3 minutes.
5. Transfer to serving bowls and serve immediately.

Chili con carne

SERVES 4

INGREDIENTS
1 tablespoon olive oil
2 cloves garlic, crushed (see page 16)
1 onion, chopped
½ teaspoon chili powder (or to taste)
1 lb (500 g) lean ground (minced) beef
1 can (14 oz/425 g) crushed tomatoes
1 tablespoon tomato paste
1 cup (8 fl oz/250 ml) Beef Stock (see page 153)
1 can (14 oz/425 g) red kidney beans, drained and rinsed
sea salt and freshly ground black pepper
crusty bread, for serving

METHOD
1. In a medium-sized frying pan over high heat, heat oil. Add garlic and onion, and fry until onion softens, about 1 minute.
2. Add chili powder and beef, and cook over medium heat, stirring, until meat changes color, about 5 minutes.
3. Add tomatoes, paste and stock, and stir. Bring to a boil, then reduce heat to low and simmer, uncovered and stirring occasionally, until thickened, about 15 minutes.
4. Add beans, stir and cook a further 10 minutes.
5. Season to taste with salt and pepper. Serve in warmed serving bowls (see page 21) with crusty bread.

VARIATION Mexican-Style Nachos
Spoon cooked chili con carne over 4 plates of warmed corn chips, sprinkle grated tasty cheese over the top, and cook under a preheated broiler (grill) until golden and melted. Serve with sour cream on the side.

Cottage pie

SERVES 4

INGREDIENTS
1 tablespoon olive oil
2 cloves garlic, crushed (see page 16)
1 onion, chopped
1 medium carrot, peeled and chopped
1 lb (500 g) ground (minced) beef or lamb
1 tablespoon Worcestershire sauce
1 tablespoon tomato paste
1 can (14 oz/425 g) crushed tomatoes
1 teaspoon dried mixed herbs
2 tablespoons chopped fresh parsley leaves
¾ cup (3 oz/90 g) frozen green peas
1 lb (500 g) potatoes, peeled and roughly chopped
2 tablespoons butter, softened
⅓ cup (3 fl oz/90 ml) milk, heated
sea salt
¼ cup (1 oz/30 g) grated tasty cheese

METHOD
1. In a large saucepan over medium–high heat, heat oil. Add garlic, onion and carrot, and cook until onion softens, 1–2 minutes. Add beef and cook, stirring, until it changes color, about 10 minutes. Stir in sauce, tomato paste, tomatoes and herbs. Bring to a boil, then reduce heat to low and cook, uncovered, until sauce thickens slightly, about 25 minutes. Add parsley and peas, and stir. Remove pan from heat and set aside.
2. Preheat oven to 350°F (180°C/Gas 4). Grease or lightly oil a 6-cup (48-fl oz/1.5-L) baking dish, or four 1½-cup (12-fl oz/375-ml) ramekins.
3. Place potatoes in a large saucepan and cover with cold water. Bring to a boil over high heat, then reduce heat to medium–high and boil until tender, about 15 minutes. Drain well.
4. Return potatoes to warm saucepan, and add butter and hot milk. Using a potato masher, mash until smooth and fluffy. (You may need to add a little more hot milk depending on potato variety.) Season with salt to taste.
5. Pour beef mixture evenly into baking dish. Top with mashed potato, spreading it evenly to cover beef mixture, then use a fork to score top.
6. Sprinkle with cheese and bake until golden brown, about 45 minutes for large baking dish or 15–20 minutes for ramekins. Spoon from baking dish onto serving plates and serve, or serve in ramekins.

Panfried steak with garlic butter

SERVES 4

INGREDIENTS
4 oz (125 g) butter, softened
2 cloves garlic, crushed (see page 16)
2 scallions (shallots/spring onions), chopped
4 tenderloin (scotch fillet or fillet) steaks, about 7 oz (220 g) each
olive oil
freshly ground black pepper

METHOD
1. Place butter in a mixing bowl and using a fork or wooden spoon, beat until soft. Add garlic and scallions, and mix until well combined.
2. Spoon butter mixture onto a piece of plastic wrap, and roll into a long cylindrical shape. Refrigerate until firm, about 15 minutes.
3. Heat a heavy-based frying pan over medium heat for 3–4 minutes until hot. Brush meat with a little olive oil and sprinkle with pepper.
4. Using tongs, place steaks into hot frying pan. Cook, without turning, until juices rise to uncooked side, 1–2 minutes. Then turn meat over and cook to your liking, a further 1 minute for medium–rare or a further 2 minutes for medium to well-done.
5. Remove steaks from pan and place on serving plates.
6. Slice garlic butter crosswise into ¼-in (6-mm) rounds and place 1 round on each steak. Serve with Green Salad (see page 86).

HINT Make a double quantity of garlic butter and store in the refrigerator for up to 1 week; you can spread it on toasted Turkish bread to make instant garlic bread, or toss it through hot pasta for a quick butter sauce.

VARIATIONS
• Herb and Garlic Butter: Substitute either 2 tablespoons chopped fresh basil leaves or fresh cilantro (fresh coriander) leaves for scallions, and blend with garlic.
• Panfried Chicken: Substitute steaks with chicken breast fillets and cook chicken until juices run clear when pierced with a skewer or fork, 4–5 minutes each side.

Hamburgers

SERVES 6

INGREDIENTS

For beef patties
1½ lb (750 g) ground (minced) beef
1 clove garlic, crushed (see page 16)
1 onion, finely chopped (see page 16)
½ cup (2 oz/60 g) fine dried white bread crumbs
2 tablespoons chopped fresh flat-leaf (Italian) parsley leaves
1 teaspoon Worcestershire sauce
1 egg, beaten

3 slices thick-cut bacon, rind removed and cut into 3-in (7.5-cm) lengths
2 tablespoons olive oil
2 onions, sliced
6 bread buns
softened butter, for spreading
1½ cups (1½ oz/45 g) mixed green salad leaves
2 tomatoes, sliced
⅓ cup (3 fl oz/90 ml) Basic Mayonnaise (see page 82)

METHOD

1. Preheat oven to 300°F (150°C/Gas 2).
2. To make beef patties: In a medium-sized mixing bowl, combine beef, garlic, onion, bread crumbs, parsley, Worcestershire sauce and egg. Using wet hands, mix until well combined. Divide mixture into 6 portions and shape into patties. Place on a plate, cover with plastic wrap and refrigerate.
3. In a nonstick frying pan over medium heat, fry bacon until golden and crisp, about 4 minutes. Remove from pan using a slotted spoon and place on a baking sheet in oven to keep warm.
4. Add oil to frying pan and cook sliced onions until golden, about 2–3 minutes. Remove from pan using a slotted spoon and place on baking sheet with bacon in oven.
5. Place beef patties in frying pan and cook until golden brown on each side, 3–4 minutes each side. Remove from pan using a slotted spoon and place on baking sheet in oven to keep warm, or place on plate and cover.

6. Meanwhile, preheat broiler (grill). Split bread buns and broil (grill) until golden.
7. Spread bread buns generously with softened butter. Top each bun base with mixed salad greens, 1 beef patty, fried onion slices, bacon pieces, tomato slices and about 1 tablespoon mayonnaise. Cover with bun tops and serve immediately.

VARIATION With Cheese
Add 1 slice tasty cheese to each hamburger when assembling fillings, or melt slice onto bun when heating in step 6.

Osso buco

This classic Italian dish is traditionally enjoyed with a fresh "gremolata." Ask your butcher to prepare the veal "osso buco" style. You will need a large flameproof casserole dish or dutch oven with lid to cook this recipe.

SERVES 4

INGREDIENTS
4 thick slices of veal shank
½ cup (2½ oz/75 g) all-purpose (plain) flour
2 tablespoons olive oil
1 onion, chopped
3 cloves garlic, roughly chopped
1 can (14 oz/425 g) crushed tomatoes
1 cup (8 fl oz/250 ml) dry white wine
1 cup (8 fl oz/250 ml) Chicken Stock (see page 154)
sea salt and freshly ground black pepper
steamed rice (see page 106), for serving

For gremolata
2 teaspoons grated lemon zest
2 cloves garlic, finely chopped
3 tablespoons finely chopped fresh parsley leaves

METHOD
1. Toss veal shins in flour to coat, shaking off any excess flour.
2. In a large flameproof casserole dish over medium heat, heat olive oil. Working in batches, fry veal shins until golden-brown on both sides, 6–7 minutes, turning halfway through cooking. Remove veal from dish and set aside. Repeat until all veal is cooked.
3. Add onion and garlic to casserole dish, and cook, stirring, until onion softens, about 1 minute.
4. Add tomatoes, wine and stock, and stir. Bring to a boil, reduce heat to low, then add veal and stir.
5. Cover and simmer over low heat until veal is tender, about 2½ hours.
6. To make gremolata: Combine all ingredients in a small bowl.
7. Serve with steamed rice and a sprinkle of gremolata if desired.

HINT Gremolata can be made in advance and stored in an airtight container in the refrigerator for 1–2 hours.

Steak sandwich with caramelized onions

SERVES 4

INGREDIENTS

For caramelized onions
3 tablespoons olive oil
4 yellow (brown) onions, thinly sliced
1 sprig fresh rosemary
1 teaspoon brown sugar
2 teaspoons balsamic vinegar

1 tablespoon olive oil
1 lb (500 g) beef fillet, cut into 4 slices
sea salt and freshly ground black pepper
8 thick slices sourdough bread
1 tablespoon whole-grain mustard
⅓ cup (3 fl oz/90 ml) Basic Mayonnaise (see page 82)
4 butter lettuce leaves, rinsed
1 tomato, sliced

METHOD
1. To make caramelized onions: In a nonstick frying pan over medium heat, heat oil. Add onions and rosemary, cover and cook, stirring frequently, until onions soften, about 10 minutes. Add brown sugar and vinegar, and cook uncovered, stirring, until onions are golden-brown, about 10 minutes. Remove pan from heat and set aside, discarding rosemary sprig.
2. Heat 1 tablespoon olive oil in a frying pan over high heat. Add steaks and cook for 2 minutes on each side. Season with sea salt and freshly ground black pepper.
3. Preheat broiler (grill) and broil (grill) bread until golden on both sides.
4. In a small bowl, combine mustard and mayonnaise. Spread on one side of each piece of toasted bread.
5. Place 4 slices bread, mayonnaise side up, on a cutting board. Top each with lettuce, tomato, steak and onions. Top with another bread slice, mayonnaise side down. Transfer to serving plates and serve immediately.

VARIATIONS
- Replace sourdough bread with Turkish bread.
- Substitute tomato slices with Slow-Roasted Tomatoes (see page 132).

Tomato, prosciutto and olive pizza

SERVES 4

INGREDIENTS

For pizza base
1 teaspoon active dry yeast
pinch white sugar
⅔ cup (5 fl oz/150 ml) warm water
2 cups (10 oz/300 g) all-purpose (plain) flour
½ teaspoon sea salt

¼ cup (2 fl oz/60 ml) olive oil
4 tomatoes, sliced
2 red onions, sliced
12 thin slices prosciutto
2 tablespoons chopped fresh oregano leaves or 2 teaspoons dried oregano
10 oz (300 g) mozzarella cheese, thinly sliced
16 small black olives
olive oil, extra, for serving
½ cup (½ oz/15 g) baby arugula (rocket) leaves, rinsed and drained

METHOD
1. In a small bowl, combine yeast, sugar and water. Cover and let stand in a warm place until mixture bubbles, about 10 minutes.
2. Place flour in a medium-sized bowl, make a well in center and add yeast mixture. Using a wooden spoon, mix to a soft dough.
3. Turn out dough onto a floured surface and knead until smooth and elastic.
4. Place dough into a clean, oiled bowl. Cover and let stand in a warm place until dough doubles in size, about 1 hour.
5. Preheat oven to 400°F (200°C/Gas 6). Line 2 baking sheets with parchment (baking) paper. Divide dough into 4 equal portions. Roll out each portion on a floured surface to form round bases about ⅛ in (3 mm) thick. Place pizza bases onto baking sheets.
6. Brush each base with olive oil and top with tomato, onion, prosciutto, oregano, cheese and olives. Bake until golden, 15–20 minutes.
7. Remove pizzas from oven, drizzle with extra olive oil, and sprinkle arugula leaves on top. Serve immediately.

Warm Thai beef salad

SERVES 4

INGREDIENTS
1 lb (500 g) sirloin (rump) steak
2 tablespoons soy sauce
2 cloves garlic, crushed (see page 16)
1 tablespoon rice wine or dry sherry
2 tablespoons olive oil
4 oz (125 g) thin egg noodles
½ English (hothouse) cucumber
4 oz (125 g) green beans, trimmed and blanched
2 small red chili peppers, seeds removed and sliced (see page 18)
3 tablespoons chopped fresh cilantro (fresh coriander) leaves
16 small fresh mint leaves
1 cup (3 oz/90 g) fresh bean sprouts, rinsed and drained
½ cup (3 oz/90 g) unsalted roasted peanuts

For dressing
2 tablespoons lime juice
2 tablespoons fish sauce
1 clove garlic, crushed (see page 16)
1 tablespoon palm sugar or brown sugar

METHOD
1. Place steak in a glass or ceramic bowl. In a small bowl, combine soy sauce, garlic and rice wine, then pour over steak and turn to coat. Cover and marinate for 30 minutes.
2. Drain steak and pat dry with paper towels.
3. In a frying pan over medium heat, heat oil. Add steak and cook until light brown on outside and pink on the inside, about 2 minutes each side. Remove from pan and let cool.
4. Thinly slice steak across grain and set aside.
5. Cook noodles as directed on package (or see page 107). Drain and rinse under cold running water after cooking, then drain well again and let cool.
6. Cut cucumber lengthwise, remove seeds using a teaspoon, then slice thinly.
7. In a medium-sized bowl, combine steak, noodles, cucumber, green beans, chili, cilantro, mint, bean sprouts and peanuts.
8. To make dressing: Place all ingredients in a screw-top jar, and shake well to combine.
9. Add dressing to salad, toss gently to combine and serve.

Chicken

Chicken is among the most versatile of all ingredients. It is widely available, economical and healthy—and is one of the few meats eaten all over the world. Chicken lends itself to most methods of cooking, and almost all parts of the chicken are commonly used.

You can roast a whole chicken; barbecue, broil (grill), pan grill or stew chicken pieces; or steam, stir-fry, panfry or poach the most tender cuts. Ground (minced) chicken may be purchased and used as a substitute for beef in dishes like lasagna, hamburgers, meatballs and bolognese sauce. Nothing is wasted, and the chicken carcass or bones may be used for making homemade stock.

Because chicken is so adaptable, you can usually substitute different cuts in recipes, depending on personal taste. Some people prefer the white breast meat to the darker thigh meat. I like to use the moist thigh meat for stirfries, curries and casseroles, and the breast fillet for pan grilling, panfrying and barbecuing. Thigh fillets are less expensive than breast fillets, and are acceptable in recipes that require chopped fillets.

Purchasing chicken

Chicken is available both fresh and frozen from supermarkets, butchers and poultry stores. Fresh chicken has a superior flavor to frozen, while free-range chicken or corn-fed chicken, recognized by its yellow skin, is considered to have a better taste and texture.

Chicken can be purchased whole or in pieces. Among the pieces are breast, tenderloin, thigh, drumstick, wing and whole leg (thigh with drumstick attached/Maryland). Many cuts are now available either with or without bone or skin. If required, ask your butcher or poultry specialist to prepare a particular cut for you.

When purchasing chicken, look for these signs of freshness:
• Fresh chicken pieces should have flesh that is light pink and moist.
• Frozen chickens should be solid and tightly wrapped.

The correct handling and storage of chicken is vitally important, as poultry is susceptible to contamination from the salmonella bacteria, which can result in food poisoning. Try to make chicken one of the last purchases when shopping, to ensure it is unrefrigerated for as short a period as possible. On warm days, use an insulated cooler (eski) to keep chicken cool while traveling home.

Storing chicken

One of the great advantages of chicken is that it is easily stored. However, care should be taken to prevent contamination by bacteria. Fresh chicken can be frozen for up to 3 months; cooked chicken for up to 2 months.

Once you get fresh chicken home, discard the original wrapping and drain any juices. Place in a single layer on a plate and loosely cover with plastic wrap. Store in the refrigerator for up to 2 days or freeze.

To freeze fresh chicken, wrap portions in freezer wrap, then place in a plastic freezer bag or container, and seal well to prevent drying out or discoloration of chicken and formation of ice crystals. Freezing the chicken in small quantities or recipe-sized portions ensures the thawing process is quicker. Label and date to ensure the chicken is eaten within its optimum recommended freezing time.

Frozen chicken should be thawed on a tray in the refrigerator. Do not thaw chicken at room temperature, or in a sink of water, as this allows bacteria to grow. Small portions of chicken may be thawed in a microwave on the "defrost" setting. However, do not defrost a whole chicken in the microwave, due to uneven thawing. Never refreeze chicken once it has been thawed. Always make sure that chicken is completely thawed before cooking.

Chicken cooking methods

How to prepare chicken for cooking

1. Rinse and pat chicken dry with paper towels. Trim excess fat and sinew.
2. If desired, skin may be removed to reduce fat content; however, cooking with skin left on does contribute to flavor and tenderness of chicken meat.
3. After preparing raw chicken, always thoroughly clean your hands, knives and cutting board before they come into contact with other foods.

How to test chicken for doneness

Chicken must be completely cooked before eating. Pink or underdone meat is not only unappealing, but also unsafe for consumption.

To test if cooked, insert a skewer or fork into the thickest part of chicken: if juices run clear, the chicken is cooked.

How to rest a roast chicken

Always let a roast chicken rest after cooking before you carve. Resting ensures the juices are retained, keeping the meat moist and tender.
1. Immediately transfer cooked chicken from pan to a warmed platter.
2. Cover with aluminum foil and let rest for 15 minutes before carving.

Basic roast chicken

Nothing beats a homemade roast chicken—whether it's full of fancy flavors or fresh and simple like this recipe. Just remember the most important step is to let the chicken rest once it is cooked, to ensure a perfectly tender result.

SERVES 6

INGREDIENTS
3¼ lb (1.6 kg) chicken
1 lemon, halved
1 fresh sprig rosemary
4 cloves garlic, unpeeled
1 tablespoon olive oil
sea salt
freshly ground black pepper

METHOD
1. Preheat oven to 400°F (200°C/Gas 6). Rinse chicken under cold water and pat dry with paper towels. Place chicken on its side in an oiled roasting pan.
2. Squeeze the juice of 1 lemon half over chicken. Place remaining lemon half, rosemary and 1 clove garlic in chicken cavity. Tuck wings behind body, then tie legs together with kitchen string. Sprinkle remaining garlic in roasting pan.
3. Brush chicken with olive oil, then season with sea salt and freshly ground black pepper.
4. Roast for 20 minutes, then baste chicken with pan juices, turn chicken over onto other side and bake a further 20 minutes.
5. Remove from oven and baste chicken with pan juices again. Turn breast side up and bake until juices run clear when chicken thigh is pierced with a skewer, a further 20 minutes (see page 59).
6. Transfer chicken to a warmed platter, cover with aluminum foil and let rest for 15 minutes (see page 59).
7. Carve chicken and serve with Chicken Gravy (see opposite).

HINT To prepare a whole chicken for roasting, remove neck and giblets from cavity; these are sometimes contained in a plastic bag.

VARIATION With Vegetables

Prepare a selection of vegetables like potato, carrot, onion and parsnip by peeling, then cutting into serving-size pieces. Place vegetable pieces into roasting pan with chicken, drizzle with olive oil, and season with sea salt and freshly ground black pepper. Roast with chicken, turning vegetables every 20 minutes, until golden and tender.

Roast chicken gravy

SERVES 4

INGREDIENTS
pan juices from roast chicken
3 tablespoons all-purpose (plain) flour
½ cup (4 fl oz/125 ml) dry white wine
2 cups (16 fl oz/500 ml) Chicken Stock (see page 158)
sea salt and freshly ground black pepper

METHOD
1. While roast chicken is resting, pour off pan juices from roasting pan, reserving about ½ cup (4 fl oz/125 ml) to make gravy.
2. Place roasting pan, with reserved pan juices, over medium heat. Sprinkle flour over base of pan and cook, stirring constantly, until flour is lightly golden, 1–2 minutes.
3. Remove pan from heat and gradually blend in wine and stock.
4. Return pan to medium heat and cook, stirring, until gravy thickens. Season with sea salt and pepper to taste, adding a little more stock if gravy is too thick.

HINT Add your choice of chopped fresh herbs to gravy.

Roast chicken with herb stuffing

SERVES 4

INGREDIENTS
3 lb (1.5 kg) chicken
4 slices whole-wheat (wholemeal) bread
4 scallions (shallots/spring onions), chopped
1 cup (1½ oz/45 g) chopped fresh flat-leaf (Italian) parsley leaves
2 teaspoons chopped fresh thyme leaves
2 teaspoons chopped fresh rosemary leaves
1 teaspoon grated lemon zest
1 teaspoon grated orange zest
sea salt and freshly ground black pepper
1 egg, lightly beaten
2 lemon slices
2 tablespoons olive oil

METHOD
1. Preheat oven to 350°F (180°C/Gas 4). Rinse chicken under cold water and pat dry with paper towels.
2. Remove crusts from bread and cut bread into small cubes.
3. In a medium-sized bowl, combine bread cubes, scallions, parsley, thyme, rosemary, lemon and orange zests, and salt and pepper to taste. Add egg and mix until well combined.
4. Using your fingertips, loosen skin from around chicken breast and insert a lemon slice on each side between skin and breast meat.
5. Spoon herb seasoning into chicken cavity. Truss chicken with string, securing wings and legs (see Basic Roast Chicken, page 60).
6. Brush base and sides of a roasting pan with oil. Place chicken in pan then brush chicken with oil.
7. Bake until juices run clear when chicken thigh is pierced with a skewer, about 1 hour and 20 minutes (see page 59). Transfer chicken to a warmed plate, cover with aluminum foil and let rest for 15 minutes (see page 59).
8. Serve hot with Crispy Roast Potatoes (see page 126) and Roast Chicken Gravy (see page 61).

Panfried chicken fillet with green peppercorn sauce

SERVES 4

INGREDIENTS
2 tablespoons butter
4 skinless chicken breast fillets
2 tablespoons all-purpose (plain) flour
1 cup (8 fl oz/250 ml) Chicken Stock (see page 154)
1 tablespoon canned green peppercorns, drained
3 tablespoons light (single) cream

METHOD
1. Preheat oven to 350°F (180°C/Gas 4). In a nonstick frying pan over medium heat, melt butter. Add chicken fillets and cook until golden on both sides, about 4 minutes each side.
2. Transfer chicken to an oiled roasting pan, and bake until cooked through, about 15 minutes.
3. Meanwhile, return frying pan to medium–high heat. Sprinkle flour into pan and cook, stirring constantly, until lightly golden, about 1 minute.
4. Remove pan from heat and gradually blend in stock. Return pan to heat and cook, stirring, until sauce thickens, 2–3 minutes. Add peppercorns and cream, reduce heat to medium–low and cook, stirring, for 2 minutes: do not let mixture boil. Remove pan from heat.
5. Place chicken on warmed serving plates (see page 21) and spoon green peppercorn sauce over. Serve with Steamed or Boiled Green Vegetables (see pages 119–121).

HINT Canned green peppercorns are available at most delicatessens or in the gourmet section of some large supermarkets.

Chicken and cashew stir-fry

Stir-frying is such a fast cooking technique that you'll have dinner ready in minutes. But make sure you have everything prepared and measured before you start cooking, and ingredients should be cut into similar sizes to ensure they cook evenly.

SERVES 4

INGREDIENTS
2 tablespoons vegetable oil
5 oz (150 g) skinless chicken breast or thigh fillet, cut into 1-in (2.5-cm) cubes
6 fresh asparagus spears, prepared (see page 17) and cut into 2-in (5-cm) pieces
1 bunch bok choy, about (13 oz/400 g), trimmed and large leaves halved
4 oz (125 g) snow peas (mange-tout), trimmed
4 oz (125 g) shiitake mushrooms, stems removed and sliced
¼ cup (2 fl oz/60 ml) Chicken Stock (see page 154)
2 teaspoons soy sauce
1 tablespoon rice wine
1 teaspoon Asian sesame oil
⅓ cup (1½ oz/45 g) unsalted roasted cashew nuts
steamed rice (see page 106), for serving

METHOD
1. In a wok or frying pan over medium heat, heat oil. Add chicken and stir-fry until golden, 4–5 minutes.
2. Increase heat to medium–high, add asparagus, bok choy, snow peas and mushrooms. Stir-fry until vegetables soften slightly, 2–3 minutes.
3. In a small bowl, combine stock, soy, rice wine and sesame oil. Add to pan and stir-fry until heated through, 1–2 minutes.
4. Remove pan from heat, add cashews and toss to combine. Serve immediately with steamed rice.

HINT Substitute button mushrooms if fresh shiitake are unavailable. You can also choose your favorite Asian greens instead of bok choy if desired.

VARIATION With Chili
Add 1 small red chili pepper, seeds removed and finely chopped (see page 17), when stir-frying chicken.

Chicken cacciatore

SERVES 4

INGREDIENTS
3 lb (1.5 kg) chicken pieces
sea salt and freshly ground black pepper
1 can (14 oz/425 g) peeled tomatoes
3 tablespoons olive oil
1 onion, chopped
3 cloves garlic, crushed (see page 16)
½ cup (4 fl oz/125 ml) dry white wine
1 cup (8 fl oz/250 ml) Chicken Stock (see page 158)
1 teaspoon sugar
1 tablespoon chopped fresh basil leaves or 1 teaspoon dried basil
2 canned flat anchovy fillets, drained and chopped (optional)
½ cup (2 oz/60 g) pitted black olives
2 tablespoons chopped fresh flat-leaf (Italian) parsley
crusty bread, for serving

METHOD
1. Preheat oven to 350°F (180°C/Gas 4). Grease an 8-cup (64-fl oz/2-L) baking dish with lid. Season chicken with sea salt and pepper.
2. In a food processor or blender, puree tomatoes until smooth. Or use a wooden spoon to push tomatoes with liquid through a sieve. Set aside.
3. In a medium-sized frying pan over medium heat, heat oil. Working in batches, add chicken pieces and cook until golden, 5–6 minutes, turning during cooking. Remove from pan using a slotted spoon and drain on paper towels. Place chicken in prepared baking dish.
4. Drain excess fat from pan, reserving 1 tablespoon in pan. Return pan to medium heat. Add onion and garlic, and cook until onion softens, about 1 minute. Add wine and stir until mixture boils for 1 minute. Add pureed tomatoes, stock, sugar and basil, and bring to a boil, stirring constantly.
5. Pour sauce over chicken pieces in baking dish, and toss to coat chicken in sauce. Cover and bake until chicken is tender, about 1 hour.
6. Remove baking dish from oven, and transfer chicken pieces to warmed serving plates (see page 21). Add anchovies, olives and parsley to remaining sauce, and stir. Spoon sauce over chicken pieces and serve with crusty bread.

HINT Do not use canned tomato puree for this recipe: it has a different flavor and is unsuitable.

Chicken in red wine with mushrooms

This well-loved French dish is known as coq au vin. Ask your butcher or poultry supplier for a combination of pieces (legs, breast, wings and thighs) on the bone. Serve with any crusty baguette or rustic-style bread loaf.

SERVES 6

INGREDIENTS
¼ cup (1½ oz/45 g) all-purpose (plain) flour
sea salt and freshly ground black pepper
4 lb (2 kg) chicken pieces
3 tablespoons olive oil
12 small white pickling onions, peeled and left whole, or 4 whole onions
    cut into quarters
3 cloves garlic, crushed (see page 16) (see page 16)
4 slices thick-cut bacon, rind removed and chopped
1½ cups (12 fl oz/375 ml) Chicken Stock (see page 154)
1½ cups (12 fl oz/375 ml) red wine
2 tablespoons brandy
¼ cup (2 oz/60 g) tomato paste
2 bay leaves
1 bouquet garni (see page 19)
6½ oz (200 g) small button mushrooms
1 tablespoon chopped fresh parsley leaves
1 baguette, sliced or torn into pieces, for serving

METHOD
1. Place flour in a plastic bag and season with salt and pepper. Add chicken pieces, one or two at a time, tossing until coated in flour. Remove from bag and shake off excess flour.
2. In a frying pan over medium heat, warm 2 tablespoons olive oil. Working in batches, add chicken pieces and cook until golden brown all over, turning to brown chicken evenly. Remove chicken from pan using a slotted spoon and set aside to drain on paper towels. Repeat until all chicken is cooked.
3. In a large heavy-based saucepan over medium heat, heat remaining 1 tablespoon olive oil. Add onions, garlic and bacon, and cook, stirring, until onions are browned, about 7 minutes.
4. In a bowl, combine stock, wine, brandy and tomato paste. Add to pan with chicken pieces and stir to combine. Bring to a boil, reduce heat to

low, then stir in bay leaves and bouquet garni. Cover and simmer for 40–45 minutes, stirring occasionally.
5. Add mushrooms to pan and stir to combine. Cover and simmer until chicken is tender, a further 10–15 minutes.
6. Place chicken and sauce in warmed serving bowls (see page 21) and sprinkle with parsley. Serve with bread slices or pieces.

Honey-soy chicken wings

These chicken wings are delicious, easy to make and inexpensive. Choose larger wings when serving these as a meal, such as with a simple green salad or steamed jasmine rice, or select smaller wings for finger food at your next party.

SERVES 4

INGREDIENTS
2 lb (1 kg) chicken wings
⅓ cup (3 fl oz/90 ml) light soy sauce
2 tablespoons lemon juice
2 tablespoons dry sherry
2 teaspoons Asian sesame oil
3 tablespoons honey
2 teaspoons peeled and grated fresh ginger

METHOD
1. Place chicken wings in a large glass or ceramic bowl.
2. In a screw-top jar, combine soy sauce, lemon juice, sherry, oil, honey and ginger. Cover and shake to mix.
3. Pour marinade over chicken wings and toss until wings are coated. Cover and refrigerate for at least 2 hours or overnight.
4. Preheat oven to 350°F (180°C/Gas 4). Place a wire rack in a roasting pan.
5. Arrange chicken wings on wire rack, reserving marinade in bowl. Bake chicken until golden and tender, basting wings with leftover marinade and turning them twice, about 30 minutes in total.
6. Remove chicken from oven. Serve warm or chilled.

HINT Marinating the wings for at least 2 hours gives them a richer flavor; marinating them overnight is even better.

Fish

Fish is a gift from the ocean. In cooking, you can do so many things with fish—from barbecue and bake to steam and, of course, sushi—and it's good for you, too. Fish is also quick to prepare, easy to cook, and can be conveniently stored in the freezer, which makes a trip to your local fish market a worthwhile, and fun, experience.

These days, however, you don't have to live near the sea to enjoy an array of fish types. A great variety of fish, and fish cuts, is conveniently available from supermarkets and seafood retailers, as well as from fish markets. Find yourself a good seafood supplier, and you'll never run out of inspiration in the kitchen.

This chapter contains some classic recipes using fish. In some cases, you can substitute the fish type suggested, for example, with a variety that is in season, but check with your fish supplier to make sure it's suitable. Remember also that the freshest fish is often best enjoyed when cooked and served simply, whether lightly rubbed with olive oil and barbecued, or pan-fried with lemon on the side.

Purchasing fish

It is important that you purchase the freshest fish, ideally, on the day you wish to eat it. Fresh fish will only keep for 1–2 days in the refrigerator.

Look for a fish supplier who has a good turnover; the fish should be presented on clean hard ice, not sitting in water. If buying whole fish, ask the fish supplier to gut and scale it; this not only extends the fish's keeping quality, but makes life much easier for you. Good fish suppliers or markets also offer a wide range of fresh cuts, or will happily prepare cuts for you as required.

Always check if the fish is fresh or frozen: avoid those which have been frozen and thawed, generally found in supermarkets, as these will be soggy and lacking in flavor. Once thawed, fish must not be refrozen and its storage life is only 1–2 days in the refrigerator.

You will, however, find high-quality fish that has been "fresh frozen." This indicates that the fish was frozen on the boat, just after it was caught, which means that when you thaw the fish yourself, it's just like fresh.

When purchasing fish, look for the following:
- Whole fish should have bright, clear eyes. Fish that is a few days old will have white and cloudy eyes.
- The flesh of whole fish should be firm.

- Fish fillets or cut pieces should be moist, with no signs of discoloration or dryness.
- Both whole fish and fish pieces should have a pleasant sea smell.

Make fish the last purchase when shopping; it should be unrefrigerated for as short a period as possible. If the weather is not cold or you're more than a few minutes from home, use an insulated cooler (eski) to keep fish cool while traveling.

Storing fish

Fish is highly perishable and must be handled and stored with care.

To store fresh fish, discard the original wrapping and drain any juices. Place in a single layer on a plate, and loosely cover with plastic wrap. Store in the refrigerator for no more than 1–2 days only, or freeze.

Freezing fresh fish

Fish should only be frozen if it is fresh: check with your fishmonger if you plan to freeze it. Remember, freezing does not save old tired food, so freeze fish when it is at its best.

To freeze fresh fish fillets: Pat fillets dry with paper towels. Wrap fillets separately in freezer wrap and place in a plastic bag or airtight container. Seal, date and label. Fish fillets may be frozen for up to 4 months.

To freeze whole fish: Scale, gut and clean fish. Remove eyes using a teaspoon and scissors. Pat dry with paper towels. Wrap in freezer wrap and place into a plastic bag. Seal, date and label. Whole fish may be frozen for up to 2 months.

Before using, frozen fish should be thawed on a tray in the refrigerator. Never thaw fish at room temperature, as this allows bacteria to grow.

Fish cooking methods

Not all fish varieties will suit all cooking methods, and some are better in pieces while others are best enjoyed whole. Remember to ask your fish supplier which cooking methods will suit the fish you choose.

How to barbecue or pan grill fish

These fast and simple cooking methods suit fish steaks, cutlets and whole fish.
1. Preheat barbecue or grill pan to high heat. Do not oil cooking plate, as this causes lots of smoke!
2. Brush fish with olive oil.

3. Place fish on barbecue or grill pan, and cook for 1–2 minutes. Turn and cook on other side until flesh flakes easily when touched with a fork, a further 1 minute.

HINT Instead of brushing with oil, fish may be marinated (see page 157) before cooking.

How to bake fish

This is a slower method of cooking that is great for whole fish, and also suits fish cutlets, steaks and thicker fillets.

For whole fish:

1. Preheat oven to 350°F (180°C/Gas 4).
2. Rub olive oil over whole fish. Use a sharp knife to make two deep cuts in the thickest part of fish on both sides. Season with sea salt and freshly ground black pepper.
3. Place fish in a baking pan, top with a few lemon slices and cover pan with aluminum foil. If fish is too large for a baking pan, wrap whole fish with lemon slices in aluminum foil and place on a baking sheet.
4. Bake until tender (flesh should look opaque and flake easily when pierced with a fork), basting fish with pan juices while cooking.

For fish fillets, steaks or cutlets:

1. Preheat oven to 350°F (180°C/Gas 4).
2. Wrap fish pieces in greased aluminum foil or parchment (baking) paper, forming into parcels. You can add a knob of butter, lemon slices, grated fresh ginger or garlic on top of fish for flavor.
3. Place parcels on a baking sheet and bake until fish is tender, 8–10 minutes.
4. Remove parcels from oven, carefully unwrap and test if fish is cooked: flesh should look opaque and flake easily when pierced with a fork.

How to deep-fry fish

This quick method of cooking suits thin fish fillets in batter, as well as small whole fish like whitebait.

1. Heat 2 cups (16 fl oz/500 ml) vegetable oil in a wok, large frying pan or saucepan over medium heat until it reaches 365°F (185°C) on a deep-frying thermometer or until a small cube of bread sizzles and browns when dropped in oil.
2. Carefully add fish, one or two pieces at a time, and cook until golden, 2–3 minutes.
3. Remove using a slotted spoon and drain on paper towels.

How to broil (grill) fish

This method of cooking suits whole fish, fish cutlets and steaks, and thicker fish fillets.

1. Preheat broiler (grill) to high heat.
2. Brush fish with melted butter or olive oil and season with salt and pepper. Place skin-side down on a baking sheet lined with aluminum foil.
3. Broil (grill) until golden, 4–5 minutes, depending on fish size. Baste during cooking to prevent drying, and turn once during cooking.
4. Using a spatula, carefully transfer cooked fish to serving plates. Serve immediately with fresh lemon wedges.

HINT Instead of brushing with olive oil, fish may be marinated (see page 157) before broiling (grilling).

How to panfry fish

This quick and easy method of cooking suits fish fillets, cutlets and steaks. If fish has skin, cook with skin-side down first. Thicker fish pieces will need longer cooking on each side. Fish steaks like tuna and salmon are usually panfried over high heat and served rare or medium (pink in center).

1. In a nonstick frying pan over medium heat, heat 1–2 tablespoons butter or good-quality olive oil.
2. Add fish and cook until fish changes color, 2–3 minutes each side, depending on thickness of fish.
3. Remove from pan using a slotted spoon and drain on paper towels. Serve immediately with fresh lemon wedges.

How to poach fish

This gentle method of cooking fish in liquid suits whole fish, fish fillets and steaks. You may need to purchase a fish poacher (kettle) to cook larger fish like whole salmon. You can poach fish either on the stove top or in the oven.

To poach fish on a stove top:
1. Half-fill a large saucepan with cold water.
2. Carefully add fish, and bring to a simmer over low heat. Cook gently until tender, 6–10 minutes per 1 lb (500 g).
3. Remove fish immediately using a slotted spoon or it will continue cooking, and drain. Serve immediately.

To poach fish in oven:
1. Preheat oven to 350°F (180°C/Gas 4). Half-fill a large fish poacher (kettle), or pan with lid, with cold water.

2. Carefully add fish and cover baking dish. Bake for about 15 minutes, depending on size of fish.
3. Remove fish poacher from oven and using a slotted spoon, transfer fish to serving plates. Serve immediately.

How to steam fish

This method of cooking suits smaller whole fish, like bream and snapper, and also fish fillets, cutlets and steaks.

1. Half-fill a medium-sized saucepan or wok with water (steamer should not touch water) and bring to a boil over high heat.
2. Arrange fish in an oiled metal or bamboo steamer, cover and place steamer over boiling water.
3. Steam until fish is opaque and flesh flakes easily when pierced with a fork, 6–8 minutes, depending on size, adding more water to pan or wok if necessary. Caution: When removing lid of steamer, tilt it away from you to avoid burning from the steam.
4. Remove steamer from pan or wok. Using a spatula, carefully transfer fish to serving plates. Serve immediately.

HINTS

- In some Asian cooking, the bamboo steamer is lined with banana leaves to add flavor and prevent food from sticking to the steamer. Use parchment (baking) paper if desired.
- Fish may be marinated (see page 157) before steaming.

How to test if fish is cooked

It is important not to overcook fish, as it will lose its delicate texture and flavor.

1. To test if cooked, pierce thickest part of fish with a fork: the flesh should look opaque and flake easily.

HINT Fresh salmon and tuna are generally cooked and served rare, with a pink center; however, these may be cooked for longer if you prefer medium.

Baked and seasoned whole fish

SERVES 4

INGREDIENTS

For seasoning
3 tablespoons olive oil
1 onion, finely chopped (see page 16)
2 ripe tomatoes, peeled and diced (see page 17)
2 cups (4 oz/125 g) fresh white bread crumbs
½ cup (2 oz/60 g) pitted black olives, finely chopped
grated zest of 1 lemon
juice from 1 lemon
⅓ cup (½ oz/15 g) chopped fresh flat-leaf (Italian) parsley
1 tablespoon chopped fresh basil leaves
sea salt and freshly ground black pepper

3 lb (1.5 kg) whole snapper, scaled and cleaned
1 teaspoon sea salt
2 tablespoons olive oil
lemon wedges, for serving
6 large fresh basil leaves, for serving

METHOD
1. Preheat oven to 400°F (200°C/Gas 6).
2. To make seasoning: In a medium-sized frying pan over medium heat, heat oil. Add onion and cook until softened, about 1 minute. Add tomatoes, stir and cook until soft and pulpy, 2–3 minutes.
3. Remove pan from heat, stir in bread crumbs, olives, lemon zest and juice, parsley, basil, and sea salt and pepper to taste. Let seasoning mixture cool.
4. Pat fish dry with paper towels, and spoon seasoning mixture into fish cavity. Using a sharp knife, make two deep slashes in thickest part of fish on both sides. Season fish with sea salt.
5. Transfer fish to an oiled baking pan, and place any remaining seasoning under fish. Drizzle fish with oil.
6. Bake, uncovered, until flesh flakes easily when pierced with a fork, 25–30 minutes.
7. Serve warm with lemon wedges. Scatter fresh basil leaves over fish.

Fish cakes

SERVES 4

INGREDIENTS

For fish cakes
2 tablespoons olive oil
1 lb (500 g) boneless and skinless salmon fillets
1 lb (500 g) potatoes, peeled and roughly chopped
grated zest of 1 lemon
1 tablespoon lemon juice
4 scallions (shallots/spring onions), chopped
2 tablespoons chopped fresh basil leaves
2 tablespoons chopped fresh flat-leaf (Italian) parsley leaves
1 egg yolk
sea salt and freshly ground black pepper to taste

½ cup (2½ oz/75 g) all-purpose (plain) flour
1½ cups (6 oz/180 g) dried bread crumbs
1 egg, beaten
2 tablespoons milk
3 tablespoons olive oil, for frying
lemon wedges, for serving
½ cup (4 fl oz/125 ml) Basic Mayonnaise (see page 82), for serving

METHOD

1. In a nonstick frying pan over medium heat, heat 2 tablespoons oil. Add salmon fillets and cook until fish flakes easily when tested with a fork, 3–4 minutes each side, depending on thickness of fish. (Salmon should be cooked to well-done.) Remove fish from pan and let cool completely.
2. Place potatoes in a medium-sized saucepan and cover with cold water. Bring to a boil over high heat, then reduce heat to medium–high and boil until tender, about 15 minutes. Drain potatoes well, return to saucepan and mash using a fork or potato masher.
3. Place cooled salmon in a large mixing bowl, and use a fork to break salmon into flakes. Add mashed potatoes, lemon zest and juice, scallions, basil, parsley and egg yolk, and season with sea salt and freshly ground black pepper. Using wet hands, mix until well combined. Refrigerate for 30 minutes.

4. Divide mixture into 8 portions and shape into patties. Place flour and bread crumbs on separate plates. Combine egg and milk in a small bowl. Coat each patty in flour, dip into egg and milk, and then coat in bread crumbs. Place on a plate and refrigerate for 30 minutes.
5. In a nonstick frying pan over medium heat, heat 3 tablespoons oil. Working in batches, cook fish cakes until golden on both sides, about 3 minutes on each side. Remove using a slotted spoon and drain on paper towels. Repeat until all fish cakes are cooked.
6. Serve warm, with lemon wedges and mayonnaise on the side.

HINTS
- You can use ready-made mayonnaise but make sure it's a good-quality egg-based one.
- Substitute fresh salmon with canned salmon if you are in a hurry. Canned salmon should be drained well before using.
- If preferred, these fish cakes may be deep-fried in hot oil.

Fish curry

SERVES 4

INGREDIENTS
2 tablespoons vegetable oil
1 onion, finely chopped (see page 16)
3 cloves garlic, crushed (see page 16)
1 teaspoon peeled and grated fresh ginger
½ teaspoon ground turmeric
1 teaspoon ground cumin
2 teaspoons ground coriander
½ teaspoon ground red chili
1 can (14 oz/425 g) crushed tomatoes
½ cup (4 fl oz/125 ml) water
1 teaspoon sea salt
1 teaspoon white sugar
1 lb (500 g) skinless firm white fish fillets, cut into 2-in (5-cm) pieces
2 tablespoons chopped fresh cilantro (fresh coriander) leaves
lemon wedges, for serving
steamed rice (see page 106), for serving

METHOD
1. In a wok or large frying pan over medium heat, heat oil.
2. Add onion, garlic, ginger, turmeric, cumin, ground coriander and ground chili, and stir-fry until fragrant, 1–2 minutes.
3. Add tomatoes, water, salt and sugar, and stir. Bring to a boil, reduce heat to low and add fish pieces.
4. Cover and simmer, stirring occasionally, until fish is opaque throughout, 8–10 minutes.
5. Spoon curry into warmed serving bowls (see page 21) and sprinkle with cilantro. Serve with lemon wedges and steamed rice.

Panfried fish with tartar sauce

White fish suitable for this recipe include bream, perch, redfish, cod, leatherjacket, hake, whiting or jackfish (trevally).

SERVES 4

INGREDIENTS
3 tablespoons all-purpose (plain) flour
sea salt and freshly ground black pepper
4 skinless white fish fillets, about 5 oz (150 g) each
1 tablespoon olive oil
2 tablespoons butter
4 lemon wedges, for serving

For tartar sauce
1 cup (8 fl oz/250 ml) Basic Mayonnaise (see page 82)
sea salt and freshly ground black pepper to taste
1 tablespoon finely chopped capers
1 tablespoon finely chopped gherkin
1 tablespoon finely chopped fresh flat-leaf (Italian) parsley leaves

METHOD
1. Place flour into a plastic bag and season with salt and pepper to taste. Add fish fillets, one or two at a time, tossing until coated in flour. Remove from bag and shake off excess flour.
2. In a medium-sized heavy-based frying pan over medium heat, heat oil. Add butter and stir until melted.
3. Working in batches, cook fish fillets until lightly golden underneath, 2–3 minutes. Using a spatula, turn fish over carefully and cook on other side until fish flakes easily when tested with a fork, about 2 minutes.
4. Serve immediately with Tartar Sauce and Green Salad (see page 86).

TARTAR SAUCE METHOD
1. In a small bowl, combine all ingredients and mix well.
2. Serve with fish, or store in a screw-top jar in the refrigerator for 1–2 days.

Salads and side breads

With the worldwide trend toward eating healthy foods, the humble salad has become a hero. First, the classic salads such as the Caesar and Waldorf started being served—and enjoyed—in cafes as lunches or light meals. Then, came a wave of "signature" creations, using a wide range of fresh and gourmet ingredients from baby spinach leaves to smoked salmon. Now, more than ever, we are making and eating fresh salads at home as meals, not just on the side.

Accelerating the salad trend is the growing recognition of fresh produce, in particular organic food. All over the world, people are discovering that well-grown food tastes fantastic as well as being good for you. Your salads will always be successful if you choose quality ingredients: fruits and vegetables in season, preferably locally-grown and organic, and always as fresh as possible. And don't forget the dressing—homemade, of course.

The great range of breads available is also encouraging us to enjoy this important staple. Many local bakers now stock a huge assortment of bread types, using various grains and seeds, in all shapes and sizes. So, more than ever, bread is convenient. Sometimes, a good hearty side bread is all the accompaniment a basic meal needs.

Purchasing salad ingredients

Choose the best-quality fresh ingredients for your salads, and use the ingredients soon after purchase to ensure their optimum texture and flavor are enjoyed.

It's easy to purchase a selection of loose mixed salad leaves (mesclun) at your greengrocer or in sealed plastic bags at the supermarket. However, it's more economical to buy the salad ingredients separately and combine the leaves at home as required. If buying premixed salad leaves, always select crisp leaves and avoid those that are wilted or discolored. If necessary, refresh the salad leaves before using (see page opposite).

Storing salad ingredients

Store salad leaves in sealed plastic bags or covered containers in the refrigerator. Do not wash until ready to use.

How to prepare salad ingredients

1. Rinse fresh salad ingredients in cold water before using to remove any grit or dirt.
2. Place in a colander or spread out on a clean kitchen towel to allow excess water to drain.
3. Trim salad leaves, then place in a sealed plastic bag or container in the refrigerator for 15 minutes before serving.

How to refresh salad leaves

1. To refresh wilted salad leaves, place in a bowl of cold water with a few ice cubes until crisp.
2. Drain in a colander or on a clean kitchen towel before using.

Basic salad dressings

There's no excuse for not making your own salad dressing—you only have to put the ingredients in a jar, shake and serve! But best of all is the flavor. Homemade salad dressings satisfy the palate.

The oil or vinegar you select for your salad dressings will depend on your budget and your taste preference. Just keep in mind, the better the quality oil or vinegar, the better the finished salad will taste!

The following salad dressings can be prepared ahead of time and stored in a screw-top jar in the refrigerator for up to 7 days. Drizzle dressing over salad just before serving: a salad becomes limp if dressed too soon.

From a basic vinaigrette (or "French dressing") to the classic mayonnaise, salad dressings will transform your favorite ingredients into something special—instantly. Use them to dress green salads, mixed leaves, ripe tomatoes, young blanched vegetables, or salads with seafood or chicken.

French dressing

This classic vinaigrette is great with salad greens or salads that include chicken, potato or egg.

MAKES ABOUT 1 CUP (8 FL OZ/250 ML)

INGREDIENTS
3 tablespoons white vinegar
¾ cup (6 fl oz/180 ml) extra virgin olive oil
½ teaspoon sugar
1 teaspoon Dijon mustard
sea salt and freshly ground black pepper to taste

METHOD
Place all ingredients into a screwtop jar, and shake well to combine.

Italian dressing

Use this on salads with seafood, chicken, pasta, tomato, basil, spinach, or roasted bell pepper (capsicum) or eggplant (aubergine).

MAKES ABOUT 1 CUP (8 FL OZ/250 ML)

INGREDIENTS
2 tablespoons white wine vinegar
2 tablespoons lemon juice
½ teaspoon sugar
1 clove garlic, crushed (see page 16)
¾ cup (6 fl oz/180 ml) extra virgin olive oil
1 tablespoon chopped mixed fresh herbs, such as basil, oregano and thyme
pinch sea salt
freshly ground black pepper

METHOD
Place all ingredients into a screw-top jar, and shake well to combine.

Balsamic vinegar dressing

This favorite is great on green salads or on salads with tomato, arugula (rocket), tuna, Parmesan or roasted bell pepper (capsicum).

MAKES ABOUT 1 CUP (8 FL OZ/250 ML)

INGREDIENTS
3 tablespoons balsamic vinegar
¾ cup (6 fl oz/180 ml) extra virgin olive oil
pinch sea salt
freshly ground black pepper

METHOD
Place all ingredients into a screw-top jar, and shake well to combine.

Basic mayonnaise

Homemade mayonnaise is delicious on salads, dolloped on steamed new potatoes, spread on sandwiches or served alongside a platter of fresh shrimp (prawns). You can make this mayonnaise in a bowl using a balloon whisk or in a food processor or blender: both methods are included here.

MAKES 1 CUP (8 FL OZ/250 ML)

INGREDIENTS
2 egg yolks
1 tablespoon lemon juice
½ teaspoon sea salt
½ teaspoon dry mustard
¾ cup (6 fl oz/180 ml) olive oil

WHISK METHOD
1. Place egg yolks, lemon juice, salt and mustard in a medium-sized bowl. Using a balloon whisk, whisk until smooth.
2. While whisking continuously, add oil a few drops at a time until at least half the oil has been added.
3. As mixture begins to thicken, add oil in a thin stream, while whisking continuously, until all oil has been added.

BLENDER OR FOOD PROCESSOR METHOD
1. Place egg yolks, lemon juice, salt and mustard into a blender or food processor, and process for 20 seconds.
2. With the motor running, gradually add oil in a steady stream and process until thick and creamy.

VARIATIONS
- Add 1 clove garlic, crushed (see page 16), or 2 teaspoons Dijon mustard, with egg yolks.
- Substitute lemon juice with lime juice, and add 1 tablespoon chopped fresh cilantro (fresh coriander) leaves.

Caesar salad

INGREDIENTS
4 thick slices white bread
3 slices thick-cut bacon, rind removed and chopped
2 tablespoons olive oil
1 romaine (cos) lettuce, leaves separated and rinsed
½ cup (2 oz/60 g) Parmesan cheese shavings (see page 19)

For dressing
3 canned flat anchovy fillets, drained
1 egg
2 tablespoons lemon juice
1 clove garlic, crushed (see page 16)
½ cup (4 fl oz/125 ml) olive oil

METHOD
1. Remove crusts from bread and cut into 1-in (2.5-cm) cubes.
2. In a nonstick frying pan over medium–high heat, cook bacon until golden and crisp, about 2 minutes. Remove from pan using a slotted spoon and drain on paper towels.
3. In same pan over medium heat, heat oil. Add bread cubes and cook, stirring constantly, until golden, 1–2 minutes. Remove from pan using a slotted spoon and drain on paper towels.
4. Tear lettuce leaves into bite-sized pieces, and arrange in a serving bowl with bacon, bread cubes and Parmesan cheese.
5. To make dressing: Place anchovies, egg, lemon juice and garlic in a food processor or blender. Process until smooth. With the motor running, add olive oil in a thin, steady stream. Process until thick and creamy.
6. Drizzle dressing over salad and serve immediately.

HINT Serve salad topped with 2 warm poached eggs (see page 32).

VARIATION Chicken Caesar Salad
In a nonstick frying pan over medium heat, heat 2 tablespoons olive oil. Add 2 skinless chicken breast fillets and cook until golden and tender, about 4 minutes each side. Transfer chicken to a baking pan and bake in a preheated 350°F (180°C/Gas 4) oven until cooked through, about 15 minutes. Let cool for 5 minutes, then slice chicken and add to salad.

Chef's salad

SERVES 4 AS A LIGHT MEAL

INGREDIENTS
2 tablespoons olive oil
12 oz (375 g) skinless chicken breast fillets
1 romaine (cos) lettuce, leaves separated and rinsed
3 tomatoes, cut into 8 wedges
5 oz (150 g) ham, cut into thin strips
3½ oz (100 g) finely sliced Swiss cheese
3 hard-boiled eggs, peeled and quartered

For dressing
⅓ cup (3 fl oz/90 ml) olive oil
2 tablespoons white wine vinegar
2 teaspoons whole-grain mustard
1 teaspoon white sugar
sea salt and freshly ground black pepper to taste

METHOD
1. Preheat oven to 350°F (180°C/Gas 4). Grease a medium-sized baking pan.
2. In a nonstick frying pan over medium heat, heat oil. Add chicken fillets and cook until golden on each side, about 4 minutes each side.
3. Transfer chicken to baking pan and bake, uncovered, until cooked through, about 15 minutes. Remove from oven and let cool for 10 minutes. Slice chicken and set aside.
4. Tear lettuce leaves into bite-sized pieces and arrange in serving bowls. Add tomatoes, ham, cheese, sliced chicken and eggs on top of lettuce, arranging them attractively in layers. Cover with plastic wrap and refrigerate until ready to serve.
5. To make dressing: Place all ingredients in a screw-top jar, and shake well to combine.
6. Drizzle dressing over salads just before serving.

HINT Add 1 red bell pepper (capsicum), seeds removed and chopped (see page 18), if desired.

Greek salad

This traditional Greek side salad is perfect with grilled seafood, chicken or lamb, or as a smart luncheon dish.

SERVES 4 AS A SIDE

INGREDIENTS
4 tomatoes, cut into quarters
2 English (hothouse) or Lebanese cucumbers, thickly sliced
½ red onion, thinly sliced
1 cup (6 oz/185 g) Kalamata olives
¼ teaspoon dried oregano leaves
1½ cups (7½ oz/225 g) cubed feta cheese

For dressing
2 teaspoons red wine vinegar
3 tablespoons extra virgin olive oil
sea salt and freshly ground black pepper to taste

METHOD
1. Arrange tomato, cucumber, onion and olives in a serving bowl. Add oregano and feta cheese.
2. To make dressing: Place all ingredients in a screw-top jar, and shake to combine.
3. Pour dressing over salad, gently toss to combine, and serve.

HINT Add 1 red bell pepper (capsicum), seeds removed and chopped (see page 18), if desired.

Green salad

The choice of salad leaves available is steadily growing—from fancy lettuces and baby spinach or arugula (rocket) to endive, mizuna and radicchio—which means that a green salad is limited only by your imagination.

SERVES 4 AS A SIDE

INGREDIENTS
about 4 cups (4 oz/125 g) mixed salad leaves
12 fresh basil leaves, torn into pieces

For dressing
2 tablespoons olive oil
2 tablespoons white wine vinegar
sea salt and freshly ground black pepper to taste
1 teaspoon whole-grain mustard

METHOD
1. In a medium bowl, combine salad leaves and basil. Cover with plastic wrap and refrigerate.
2. To make dressing: Place all ingredients in a screw-top jar and shake well to combine.
3. Just before serving, pour dressing evenly over salad leaves and gently toss to combine.

HINT You can prepare this salad 1–2 hours prior to serving and keep it covered in the refrigerator; however, to ensure that it stays crisp, dress the salad just before serving.

Potato salad

For best results, choose low-starch potato varieties such as Sebago, Desiree, Rose Fir, white rose or fingerling (kipfler). If preferred, scrub potato skins clean under cold running water and leave on instead of peeling.

SERVES 4 AS A SIDE

INGREDIENTS
3 lb (1.5 kg) potatoes, peeled and cut into 1-in (2.5-cm) cubes
2 tablespoons cider vinegar
1 cup (8 fl oz/250 ml) Basic Mayonnaise (see page 82)
3 scallions (shallots/spring onions), sliced
2 tablespoons chopped fresh flat-leaf (Italian) parsley
sea salt and freshly ground black pepper

METHOD
1. Place potatoes in a large saucepan and cover with cold water. Bring to a boil over high heat, then reduce heat to medium–high and simmer, uncovered, until just tender, 8–10 minutes.
2. Drain well, then spread potato on a baking sheet and sprinkle with vinegar. Let cool for 10 minutes, then refrigerate until cold.
3. In a large bowl, combine potato, mayonnaise, scallions, parsley, and salt and pepper to taste. Mix gently.
4. Spoon into a serving bowl. Cover and refrigerate until well chilled before serving.

VARIATIONS
- For added flavor, mix 2 teaspoons whole-grain mustard into mayonnaise before using in recipe.
- Add 1 hard-boiled egg, chopped, to bowl with other ingredients before combining.

Salad Niçoise

For best results, choose low-starch potato varieties such as Sebago, Desiree or fingerling (kipfler).

SERVES 4 AS A SIDE

INGREDIENTS
4 medium potatoes
8 oz (250 g) green beans, trimmed
1 can (12 oz/375 g) tuna in olive oil, drained and flaked
2 tomatoes, cut into wedges
16 small black olives
1 red onion, sliced
2 cups (2 oz/60 g) mixed green salad leaves
2 hard-boiled eggs, quartered
8 canned flat anchovy fillets, drained and cut lengthwise

For dressing
2 tablespoons olive oil
1 tablespoon lemon juice
sea salt and freshly ground black pepper to taste

METHOD
1. Scrub unpeeled potatoes under cold running water, then cut each into quarters. Place potatoes in a medium-sized saucepan and cover with cold water. Bring to a boil over high heat, then reduce heat to medium–high and simmer, uncovered, until just tender, 10–12 minutes. Drain well and set aside.
2. Half-fill clean medium-sized saucepan with water and bring to a boil over high heat. Add beans and cook just until tender-crisp and color changes, becoming brighter, about 1 minute. Using a slotted spoon, quickly remove beans from saucepan and immediately plunge in a large bowl of ice water to stop cooking process. Let beans cool completely in ice water, then drain well.
3. To make dressing: Place all dressing ingredients in a screw-top jar and shake well to combine.
4. In a large mixing bowl, combine warm potatoes, beans, tuna, tomatoes, olives and onion. Add dressing and toss gently to mix.
5. Arrange salad leaves on a serving platter or 4 serving plates. Top with potato mixture. Arrange egg and anchovies on top. Serve immediately.

Tabbouleh

INGREDIENTS
¾ cup (4 oz/125 g) bulgur (burghul)
2 cups (3 oz/90 g) chopped fresh flat-leaf (Italian) parsley
½ cup (¾ oz/20 g) chopped fresh mint
½ cup (¾ oz/30 g) chopped scallions (shallots/spring onions)
3 tomatoes, chopped
1 teaspoon sea salt
freshly ground black pepper to taste
¼ cup (2 fl oz/60 ml) extra virgin olive oil
⅓ cup (3 fl oz/90 ml) lemon juice

METHOD
1. Place bulgur in a medium-sized bowl. Cover with hot water and let stand at room temperature for 20 minutes. Drain well through a fine sieve.
2. In a large bowl, combine bulgur, parsley, mint, scallions, tomato, salt and pepper to taste.
3. Place oil and lemon juice in a screw-top jar, cover and shake well to combine.
4. Pour dressing over salad and toss gently to mix. Serve immediately.

HINT Bulgur (burghul) is available in the health food or grain section of your supermarket or from delicatessens or health food stores.

VARIATION For a tangy flavor, add the grated zest of 1 lemon to other ingredients before mixing.

Waldorf salad

INGREDIENTS
3 red apples
⅓ cup (3 fl oz/90 ml) lemon juice
4 celery stalks, sliced
½ cup (2 oz/60 g) roughly chopped walnuts
4 butter lettuce leaves, rinsed, for serving

For dressing
2 egg yolks
2 teaspoons lemon juice
1 teaspoon Dijon mustard
¾ cup (6 fl oz/180 ml) olive oil
1 tablespoon warm water
sea salt and freshly ground black pepper

METHOD
1. To make dressing: Place egg yolks, lemon juice and mustard in a blender or food processor, and process for 20 seconds.
2. With the motor running, gradually add olive oil in a steady stream. Process until thick and creamy. Transfer to a small mixing bowl.
3. Stir in warm water and salt and pepper to taste. Cover and refrigerate.
4. Core and roughly chop apples: do not remove peel.
5. In a medium-sized bowl, combine apple and lemon juice, and toss until apple is well coated in juice. (This prevents the apple from turning brown.)
6. Add celery, walnuts and dressing, and toss to combine.
7. Line 4 small salad bowls with 1 lettuce leaf each. Place salad on lettuce in bowl and serve.

HINTS
- For a delicious lunch, place Waldorf salad on a buttered crusty bread roll and top with shredded cold roast chicken meat.
- Use 2 green apples and 2 red apples for a change in taste and color.

Warm penne and tomato salad

SERVES 4 AS A LIGHT MEAL

INGREDIENTS
12 oz (375 g) penne pasta
⅓ cup (3 fl oz/90 ml) olive oil
4 cloves garlic, finely chopped
6 tomatoes, seeds removed and roughly chopped (see page 17)
1 cup (1 oz/30 g) baby arugula (rocket) leaves, rinsed
sea salt and freshly ground black pepper

METHOD
1. Bring a large saucepan of water to a boil over high heat. Add pasta and cook until tender, 10–12 minutes.
2. Drain pasta and rinse under warm water (this prevents pasta from sticking together).
3. In a medium-sized bowl, combine olive oil, garlic and tomatoes. Add warm pasta, arugula, and salt and pepper to taste. Quickly toss to combine and serve immediately.

VARIATIONS
If desired, you can add favorite ingredients to this salad before tossing to combine. For example, try any of the following:
- 12 black olives, pitted
- 3 canned flat anchovy fillets, drained and chopped
- 1 medium-sized fresh red chili pepper, seeds removed and chopped (see page 18)
- 1 can (6 oz/185 g) tuna in olive oil, drained and flaked

Herb-garlic bread

SERVES 6–8 AS AN ACCOMPANIMENT

INGREDIENTS
1 cup (8 oz/250 g) unsalted butter, softened
6 cloves garlic, crushed
3 tablespoons chopped fresh flat-leaf (Italian) parsley leaves
2 tablespoons mixed chopped fresh herbs, such as thyme, chervil, tarragon
2 teaspoons lemon juice
2 baguettes

METHOD
1. Preheat oven to 400°F (200°C/Gas 6).
2. Place butter in a medium-sized bowl and, using an electric mixer or fork, beat until soft and creamy. Add garlic, parsley, herbs and lemon juice. Mix until well combined.
3. Using a serrated knife, cut each baguette crosswise into thick slices. Spread butter on each side of bread slices, and reform slices into a loaf. Wrap in aluminum foil, place on a baking sheet and bake for 15 minutes.
4. Remove from oven and open foil to expose top of bread. Return to oven and bake until golden, a further 10 minutes. Serve immediately.

Tomato bruschette

INGREDIENTS
8 thick slices sourdough or wood-fired bread
extra virgin olive oil
3 cloves garlic
6 tomatoes, seeds removed and roughly chopped (see page 17)
sea salt and freshly ground black pepper
12 fresh basil leaves, torn

METHOD
1. Preheat broiler (grill) to high heat.
2. Brush both sides of bread slices with olive oil and broil (grill) until golden on both sides.
3. Place garlic on a cutting board and crush (see page 16). Rub one side of each bread slice with crushed garlic cloves.
4. Place chopped tomato in a mixing bowl, and season to taste with plenty of salt and pepper.
5. Spoon tomato on top of bread and scatter with basil. Drizzle with olive oil and serve immediately.

Pasta

Pasta—the famous food of Italy—has become a modern staple worldwide. From spaghetti and fettuccine to spirals and tiny farfalle, and all the many shapes and sizes in between, pasta is served in the finest restaurants, in al fresco cafes, and, of course, at home among family and friends.

Pasta is quick, nutritious, satisfying and, best of all, once you've mastered the basic techniques you'll always be able to make a delicious meal. Simply open your fridge or pantry, and you'll usually find many ingredients that can be used to make a pasta dish. You can also make some pasta sauces in advance, and store them, to be enjoyed at your convenience.

This chapter includes a range of basic sauces, but feel free to experiment with the flavors. Pasta is a creative food, so let your taste buds rule. Adding a twist to a classic is how favorite pasta dishes are made!

Pasta cooking methods

Recommended servings for pasta
As a general rule, for each serving, allow 2½–4 oz (75–125 g) uncooked dried pasta, or 4–5½ oz (125–175 g) uncooked fresh pasta.

How to cook fresh pasta
1. Fill a large saucepan two-thirds full with water, and add 1 tablespoon olive oil (to prevent pasta from sticking together). Bring to a rapid boil over high heat.
2. Add pasta and stir to separate.
3. Boil, uncovered, until al dente, 2–4 minutes (depending on pasta type).

How to cook dried pasta
1. Fill a large saucepan two-thirds full with water, and add 1 tablespoon olive oil (to prevent pasta sticking together). Bring to a rapid boil over high heat.
2. Add pasta and stir to separate.
3. Boil, uncovered, until al dente, 10–14 minutes (depending on pasta type).

HINT Make sure the water is boiling rapidly before you add the pasta.

How to test if pasta is al dente

The term al dente is Italian for "to the tooth," and it is used to describe perfectly cooked pasta, which is tender but still firm.

To test, remove a piece of pasta from pan and taste. It should be cooked through, with no signs of chalkiness in the center, but still firm in texture.

How to drain cooked pasta

1. When pasta is al dente, drain immediately in a colander or sieve.
2. If serving hot, use immediately: do not rinse (the starch on cooked pasta helps the sauce to stick to it). If using pasta cold, rinse under warm running water followed by cold running water, to remove excess starch, then drain well: this will prevent pasta from sticking together.

How to serve pasta

Always have the sauce prepared before you start cooking the pasta, to ensure the pasta is served piping hot.

1. After draining, return hot pasta to the saucepan it was cooked in. (Only rinse if using cooked pasta cold.)
2. Serve cooked pasta immediately, to prevent it from becoming sticky.

How to reheat cooked pasta

1. Place cooked pasta in a colander or sieve over a large saucepan.
2. Pour boiling water over pasta into pan and, using a fork, separate pasta pieces in water. Cover for 5 minutes.
3. Carefully lift colander or sieve from pan to drain pasta.

How to store cooked pasta

1. Drain cooked pasta in colander or sieve and rinse under warm running water followed by cold running water, then drain well.
2. Add a little olive oil and toss to coat pasta.
3. Keep in a sealed container in the refrigerator for up to 3 days.

Basic bolognese sauce

This classic sauce can be served simply with pasta of your choice, or used in other dishes such as Beef and Ricotta Lasagna (see page 98).

SERVES 4 WITH PASTA

INGREDIENTS
2 tablespoons olive oil
1 onion, chopped
3 cloves garlic, crushed (see page 16)
2 carrots, peeled and chopped
2 slices thick-cut bacon, rind removed and chopped
1 lb (500 g) ground (minced) beef
½ cup (4 fl oz/125 ml) red wine
1 can (14 oz/425 g) crushed tomatoes
½ cup (4 fl oz/125 ml) Beef Stock (see page 153)
2 tablespoons tomato paste
1 bay leaf
pinch white sugar
2 tablespoons chopped fresh flat-leaf (Italian) parsley leaves
sea salt and freshly ground black pepper

METHOD
1. In a large frying pan or saucepan over medium–high heat, heat oil. Add onion, garlic and carrots, and cook until onion softens, 1–2 minutes.
2. Add bacon and beef, and cook, stirring, until meat browns.
3. Stir in wine and let boil for 2–3 minutes.
4. Add tomatoes, stock, tomato paste, bay leaf and sugar, and stir. Bring to a boil over high heat. Reduce heat to low and simmer, uncovered, until sauce has thickened, 30–40 minutes.
5. Add parsley to sauce and stir, then season with salt and pepper to taste. Serve hot over cooked pasta.

HINT Bolognese sauce will keep in a sealed container for 3 days in the refrigerator or for up to 2 months in the freezer.

Spaghetti bolognese

SERVES 4

INGREDIENTS
12–14 oz (375–500 g) spaghetti
1 quantity Basic Bolognese Sauce (see opposite), hot
½ cup (2 oz/60 g) freshly grated Parmesan cheese
crusty bread, for serving

METHOD
1. Bring a large saucepan of water to a boil. Add spaghetti and cook until tender, 10–12 minutes. Drain well using a sieve or colander.
2. Arrange cooked spaghetti on serving plates and top with piping-hot sauce. Serve with grated Parmesan cheese and crusty bread.

HINT You can use any pasta of your choice instead of spaghetti, such as fettucine, penne or macaroni.

VARIATION Chicken Bolognese
Follow recipe for Bolognese Sauce (see opposite) using ground (minced) chicken breast meat and chicken stock instead of ground beef and beef stock.

Beef and ricotta lasagna

SERVES 6

INGREDIENTS

2½ cups (1½ lb/750 g) ricotta cheese
½ cup (2 oz/60 g) grated Parmesan cheese
2 teaspoons dried oregano leaves
3 tablespoons chopped fresh flat-leaf (Italian) parsley leaves
2 eggs, beaten
sea salt and freshly ground black pepper
12 oz (375 g) fresh lasagna sheets
1 lb (500 g) mozzarella cheese, thinly sliced
1 quantity Basic Bolognese Sauce (see page 96)

METHOD

1. Preheat oven to 350°F (180°C/Gas 4). Grease a deep 12-in x 10-in (30-cm x 25-cm) baking pan or dish.
2. In a medium-sized mixing bowl, combine ricotta and Parmesan cheeses, oregano, parsley, eggs, and salt and pepper to taste. Mix until well combined.
3. Arrange a layer of lasagna sheets over base of baking pan. Spread half of cheese mixture on top. Cover with half of mozzarella cheese and then half of bolognese sauce.
4. Place another layer of lasagna sheets in baking pan and spread remaining half of cheese mixture on top. Cover with remaining half of sauce and finish with mozzarella on top.
5. Bake until golden on top, 40–45 minutes. Remove from oven and let stand for 15 minutes.
6. Cut lasagna into squares for serving. Serve with Green Salad (see page 86) and Herb-Garlic Bread (see page 92).

HINT If preferred, you can use dried lasagna sheets instead of fresh; follow preparation/cooking instructions on package before using in recipe.

Fettuccine carbonara

The heat of al dente pasta cooks the egg yolks in this recipe so make sure you put the cooked and drained fettuccine back into the saucepan, covered, to keep it warm.

SERVES 4

INGREDIENTS
12–14 oz (375–500 g) fettuccine
6 slices thick-cut bacon, rind removed and cut into narrow strips
3 oz (90 g) button mushrooms, thinly sliced
¾ cup (6 fl oz/180 ml) light (single) cream
4 egg yolks
sea salt and freshly ground black pepper to taste
½ cup (2 oz/60 g) freshly grated Parmesan cheese
2 tablespoons chopped fresh flat-leaf (Italian) parsley leaves

METHOD
1. Bring a large saucepan of water to a boil. Add fettuccine and cook until al dente, about 10 minutes.
2. Meanwhile, heat a frying pan over medium–high heat. Add bacon and cook, stirring, until crisp. Then add mushrooms and cook, stirring, until soft, about 3–4 minutes. Remove from pan and set aside.
3. Drain cooked fettuccine using a sieve or colander, return immediately to hot saucepan and cover.
4. In a mixing bowl, combine cream, egg yolks, and Parmesan cheese, and season with salt and pepper. Add to hot fettuccine in pan and toss until well combined.
5. Add bacon, mushrooms and parsley, and toss to combine. Serve immediately.

Macaroni and cheese

The easiest of comfort foods, this recipe is also a great way to use leftover cooked pasta, such as penne or shells.

SERVES 4

INGREDIENTS
12 oz (375 g) macaroni
2 tablespoons butter
2 tablespoons all-purpose (plain) flour
1 teaspoon dry mustard powder
2 cups (16 fl oz/500 ml) milk
sea salt and freshly ground black pepper to taste
¾ cup (3 oz/90 g) grated Gruyère or tasty cheese
¼ cup (1 oz/30 g) grated Parmesan cheese

METHOD
1. Preheat oven to 350°F (180°C/Gas 4). Grease a 6-cup (48-fl oz/1.5-L) baking dish.
2. Bring a large saucepan of water to a boil. Add macaroni and cook until al dente, 8–10 minutes. Drain well using a sieve or colander and set aside.
3. In a medium-sized saucepan over low heat, melt butter. Add flour and mustard and cook, stirring, until mixture bubbles, about 1 minute.
4. Remove from heat and gradually add milk, stirring constantly. Return pan to a medium heat and cook, stirring, until sauce boils and thickens. Season with salt and pepper.
5. Add Gruyère cheese and cook, stirring, until melted. Remove from heat, add cooked macaroni and stir to combine.
6. Spoon macaroni and cheese mixture evenly into baking dish, and sprinkle with Parmesan cheese. Bake until golden, about 15 minutes.
7. Remove from oven, and serve hot in warmed bowls (see page 21).

VARIATION Add 6 oz (185 g) ham, chopped or 2 hard-boiled eggs, chopped, to cheese sauce, before combining with macaroni and baking.

Neapolitan sauce

This basic tomato sauce has as many uses as it has variations: try it with chopped olives scattered over just before serving, a sprinkle of chili, or simply with shavings of Parmesan cheese (see page 19).

SERVES 4 WITH PASTA

INGREDIENTS
1 tablespoon olive oil
1 onion, chopped
2 cloves garlic, crushed (see page 16)
2 cans (14 oz/425 g each) crushed tomatoes
sea salt and freshly ground black pepper
2 tablespoons chopped fresh basil leaves
2 tablespoons chopped fresh flat-leaf (Italian) parsley leaves

METHOD
1. In a medium-sized saucepan over medium heat, heat oil. Add onion and garlic, and cook, stirring, until onion softens, about 1 minute.
2. Add tomatoes and salt and pepper to taste, and stir. Bring to a boil, reduce heat to low and simmer, uncovered, until sauce thickens slightly, about 15 minutes. Remove from heat and stir in basil and parsley.
3. Serve hot with cooked pasta.

HINT Neapolitan sauce will keep in a sealed container for 3 days in the refrigerator or for up to 4 months in the freezer.

VARIATIONS
If desired, add any of the following ingredients when stirring in fresh herbs:
• 12 black olives, pitted
• 1 medium-sized fresh red chili pepper, seeds removed and chopped (see page 18)
• 1 tablespoon salted capers, rinsed and drained

Pesto sauce

Make a double quantity of pesto, store it in the refrigerator and you'll always have a flavorsome ingredient to use on pizza bases and sandwiches; to serve with barbecued beef, lamb and chicken; and for instant pasta meals.

SERVES 4 WITH PASTA

INGREDIENTS
¼ cup (1 oz/30 g) pine nuts
1 cup (1 oz/30 g) firmly packed fresh basil leaves
3 cloves garlic, crushed (see page 16)
½ cup (4 fl oz/125 ml) olive oil
2 tablespoons freshly grated Parmesan cheese

METHOD
1. Place pine nuts, basil, garlic and about 1 tablespoon olive oil in a food processor or blender. Process until roughly chopped.
2. With motor running, add remaining olive oil in a steady stream. Process until well combined. Transfer to a small mixing bowl.
3. Add Parmesan cheese and stir to mix well.
4. Toss pesto through cooked pasta and serve.

HINTS
- Pesto can be stored in an airtight jar in the refrigerator for up to 1 week.
- For added flavor, toast pine nuts in a hot frying pan (see page 16) or under a preheated broiler (grill) before using in recipe.

Spaghetti with olive oil and garlic sauce

This is pasta at its basic best, using stocked ingredients from your kitchen. Use your best olive oil here, as the quality determines how the finished dish will taste.

SERVES 4

INGREDIENTS
12 oz (375 g) spaghetti
½ cup (4 fl oz/125 ml) extra virgin olive oil
4 cloves garlic, finely chopped (see page 16)
2 tablespoons chopped fresh flat-leaf (Italian) parsley leaves
sea salt and freshly ground black pepper to taste

METHOD
1. Bring a large saucepan of water to a boil. Add spaghetti and cook until al dente, 8–10 minutes. Drain well using a sieve or colander, return immediately to saucepan, and cover.
2. In a medium frying pan over low heat, heat oil. Add garlic and cook gently until garlic flavors oil, 5–6 minutes; do not let garlic brown.
3. Remove from heat, add parsley and stir. Season with salt and pepper.
4. Pour warm garlic-oil mixture over spaghetti and toss to coat. Serve immediately.

HINT Substitute spaghetti with pasta of your choice such as penne or fettuccine.

VARIATION With Chili
Add 1–2 large fresh red chili peppers, seeds removed and finely chopped (see page 17), to oil with garlic.

Spaghetti and meatballs

This easy version of a pasta classic is one of my family's all-time favorites.

SERVES 4

INGREDIENTS

For meatballs
1 lb (500 g) ground (minced) beef
1 onion, finely chopped (see page 16)
2 cloves garlic, crushed (see page 16)
2 tablespoons chopped fresh flat-leaf (Italian) parsley leaves
½ cup (1 oz/30 g) fresh bread crumbs
2 teaspoons Worcestershire sauce
¼ cup (1½ oz/45 g) all-purpose (plain) flour
2 tablespoons olive oil

For sauce
1 tablespoon olive oil
1 onion, finely chopped (see page 16)
4 cloves garlic, crushed (see page 16)
1 small fresh red chili pepper, seeds removed and finely chopped
  (see page 18) (optional)
2 cans (14 oz/425 g each) crushed tomatoes
2 tablespoons tomato paste
1 teaspoon white sugar
½ cup (4 fl oz/125 ml) Beef Stock (see page 153)
sea salt and freshly ground black pepper

12 oz (375 g) spaghetti
½ cup (2 oz/60 g) grated Parmesan cheese, for serving

METHOD
1. To make meatballs: In a mixing bowl, combine beef, onion, garlic,
   parsley, bread crumbs and Worcestershire sauce. Place flour on a plate.
   Using clean wet hands, mix meatball mixture until well combined. Take
   about 1 tablespoon of mixture, roll into a ball, and toss in flour to coat.
   Repeat with remaining meatball mixture.
2. In a frying pan over medium heat, heat oil. Working in batches, cook
   meatballs until golden brown, about 4–5 minutes. Remove using a

slotted spoon and drain on paper towels. Repeat until all meatballs are cooked.

3. To make sauce: In a frying pan over medium heat, heat oil. Add onion, garlic and chili pepper, and cook, stirring, until onion softens, about 1 minute. Add tomatoes, tomato paste, sugar and stock, and bring to a boil.

4. Reduce heat to low and add meatballs. Cook, uncovered, for 15 minutes, turning meatballs occasionally. Season with salt and pepper to taste.

5. Bring a large saucepan of water to a boil. Add spaghetti and cook until al dente, 8–10 minutes. Drain well using a sieve or colander.

6. Place spaghetti in warmed serving bowls (see page 21) and top with meatballs and sauce. Sprinkle with grated Parmesan cheese and serve.

HINT Making the meatballs and sauce at least a day ahead will give this dish a richer flavor—simply reheat the meatballs and sauce together while cooking the pasta.

Rice, noodles, lentils and couscous

Whenever we think of the "basics" in food, the comforting grains come to mind. Rice, noodles, lentils and their like are traditional staples that have stood the test of time. All over the world, grains form the basis of most diets—they're economical, highly nutritious, adaptable and, best of all, easy to prepare.

These days, the range of grain foods available on supermarket shelves is infinite. You'll find rice in all its glorious forms; noodles fresh, frozen and dried; a colorful array of lentils and legumes; as well as couscous, oats, barley and other grains. And if you keep your pantry well stocked with these staples, you'll always have a fast and filling meal on hand.

In this chapter, you'll find some of the classic rice and noodle dishes, such as Basic Risotto and Pad Thai Noodles. But don't forget that simply cooked grains, like steamed rice or couscous, can also be the perfect accompaniment to countless main dishes.

Cooking methods

How to cook rice
The most common method for cooking rice is simply to steam it. You will need 1 cup (7 oz/220 g) raw white rice to yield 3 cups (15 oz/470 g) cooked white rice; and 1 cup (7 oz/220 g) raw brown rice to yield 3½ cups (18 oz/560 g) cooked brown rice. Allow about ½ cup (3½ oz/100 g) raw rice per person. You will need a heavy-based saucepan with a tight-fitting lid to cook rice: choose a medium-size for 4–6 servings, and larger if cooking for more.

To steam rice (absorption method):
1. Place raw rice into a sieve and rinse under cold running water until water runs clear.
2. Place rice into saucepan and add a little salt.
3. Add enough cold water to cover rice by ¾ in (2 cm). (Some cooks measure by resting the tip of their index finger on top of the rice, adding just enough water to touch the first joint.)

4. Place saucepan over high heat and bring to a boil. Cook until craters form on rice surface and water has evaporated, 10–12 minutes.
5. Cover immediately with a tight-fitting lid and reduce heat to low. Cook until all water has been absorbed and rice is tender, about 20 minutes. Do not lift lid during cooking, as this allows steam to escape.

HINT Cooked rice may be stored in a sealed container in the refrigerator for up to 5 days or frozen for up to 2 months.

How to cook couscous

Hot couscous can be served as a side with meat, fish or chicken dishes. It can also be used cold in nutritious and delicious salads—try it tossed with blanched or roasted vegetables, chopped fresh mint and parsley leaves, olive oil and lemon juice. You will need about 2 cups (12 oz/375 g) uncooked couscous for 4 servings.
1. Place couscous into a heatproof bowl.
2. Add 2 cups (16 fl oz/500 ml) boiling Chicken Stock (see page 154) or water and stir. Cover and let stand until all liquid has been absorbed.
3. Stir couscous with a fork, adding 1 tablespoon softened butter, sea salt and freshly ground black pepper to taste.
4. Add chopped herbs of your choice and a squeeze of fresh lemon juice, and stir through.

How to cook noodles

Noodles are available in an endless array of shapes, sizes and varieties. Always check the package for recommended soaking or cooking instructions. There are two common methods of preparing noodles.

To cook fresh or dried noodles:
1. Bring a large saucepan of water to a boil over high heat.
2. Add noodles and cook until tender, 5–8 minutes, depending on type of noodle.
3. Drain well using a sieve.

To soak dried noodles:
1. Place noodles in a heatproof bowl and cover with boiling water.
2. Let soak until noodles are soft, 8–10 minutes.
3. Drain well using a sieve.

HINT Store dried noodles in an airtight container in the pantry. Keep fresh noodles in the refrigerator; refer to the use-by date on the package.

How to cook lentils

The various lentils are easily identified by their color. Brown lentils are generally used for soups, casseroles and salads because they hold their shape once cooked. Red lentils (actually red-orange) have a slight spicy flavor and are used in soups and purees, as they have a soft, creamy texture once cooked. Gray or Puy lentils, traditionally used in French cooking, are much smaller than the others. They have a wonderful flavor and retain a good texture but are expensive.

1. Rinse lentils and drain well before cooking. Lentils do not require overnight soaking. Use as directed in recipe, or cook as described here.
2. Half-fill a heavy-based saucepan with water and bring to a boil over medium heat.
3. Add lentils and cook until tender, 15–20 minutes.
4. Remove from heat and drain in a sieve or colander. Serve hot or cold.

Basic risotto

One of the all-time great comfort foods, risotto is also one of the essential basics. And once you've mastered the technique, you can get creative and devise endless variations.

SERVES 4

INGREDIENTS
4½ cups (36 fl oz/1.1 L) Chicken Stock (see page 154)
1 cup (8 fl oz/250 ml) dry white wine
1 tablespoon olive oil
1 tablespoon butter
1 onion, chopped
1 clove garlic, crushed (see page 16)
2 cups (14 oz/425 g) Arborio rice
sea salt and freshly ground black pepper
1 tablespoon butter, extra
½ cup (2 oz/60 g) grated Parmesan cheese
2 tablespoons chopped fresh flat-leaf (Italian) parsley leaves

METHOD
1. In a medium-sized saucepan over medium heat, heat stock and wine and bring to a boil. Reduce heat to low and let simmer.
2. In a large heavy-based saucepan over medium heat, heat oil and butter. Add onion and garlic, and cook until onion softens, about 1 minute.
3. Add rice and cook, stirring, until translucent, about 2 minutes.
4. Slowly add 1 cup (8 fl oz/250 ml) hot stock, stirring constantly until absorbed, 6–8 minutes.
5. Continue adding stock a cupful at a time until rice is soft and creamy, 20–25 minutes in total. Rice grains should be firm but tender. Season with sea salt and black pepper to taste.
6. Remove pan from heat and add extra 1 tablespoon butter and Parmesan cheese. Gently stir to combine, then cover and let stand 5 minutes.
7. Spoon risotto into warmed serving bowls or plates (see page 21), and serve sprinkled with parsley.

VARIATION With Lemon
Add the grated zest of 1 lemon with the extra butter and Parmesan cheese.

Couscous salad

This versatile grain salad is great served warm or chilled with lamb, chicken or fish. For vegetarians, replace chicken stock with a vegetable alternative.

SERVES 4 AS A SIDE

INGREDIENTS

1¼ lb (650 g) sweet potatoes or yams (kumara), peeled and
   cut into 1-in (2.5-cm) cubes
3 zucchini (courgettes), cut into 1-in (2.5-cm) slices
3 cloves garlic, finely chopped (see page 16)
sea salt
3 tablespoons olive oil
1 cup (8 fl oz/250 ml) Chicken Stock (see page 154)
1 cup (6 oz/185 g) instant couscous
3 tablespoons chopped fresh mint leaves
2 tablespoons chopped fresh flat-leaf (Italian) parsley leaves
8 cherry tomatoes, quartered

For dressing
3 tablespoons lemon juice
3 tablespoons olive oil
sea salt and freshly ground black pepper to taste

METHOD

1. Preheat oven to 400°F (200°C/Gas 6). Grease or line a baking pan with parchment (baking) paper. Arrange sweet potato and zucchini in a single layer in pan. Sprinkle with garlic and sea salt. Drizzle with olive oil.
2. Bake vegetables until golden and tender, 20–25 minutes, turning at least twice during cooking. Remove from oven and set aside.
3. In a medium-sized saucepan over high heat, bring stock to a boil.
4. Place couscous in a heatproof bowl and add boiling stock. Stir with a fork, cover and let stand until all liquid has been absorbed. Stir again to separate grains.
5. In a large bowl, combine warm couscous and roasted vegetables with mint, parsley and tomatoes.
6. To make dressing: Place ingredients in a screw-top jar and shake to mix.
7. Pour dressing over salad. Toss to combine. Adjust seasoning with salt and pepper. Serve warm, or refrigerate in an airtight container for 1–2 days.

Fried rice

This all-time favorite is best made with leftover cooked rice, at least a day old, because the cold rice grains don't stick together when fried. If cooking rice for this recipe, you'll need 1 cup (7 oz/220 g) raw rice to make about 3 cups cooked (see page 106). Drain cooked rice, spread on a baking pan, cover with paper towels and refrigerate overnight. Before using cold rice, wet your hands and separate the grains.

SERVES 4

INGREDIENTS
3 tablespoons vegetable oil
2 eggs, beaten
4 scallions (shallots/spring onions), chopped
1 clove garlic, crushed (see page 16)
2 teaspoons peeled and grated fresh ginger
2 celery stalks, chopped
4 oz (125 g) Chinese barbecued pork, chopped
4 oz (125 g) small cooked shrimp (prawns), peeled
½ cup (2½ oz/75 g) frozen green peas, thawed
3 cups (15 oz/470 g) cold cooked long-grain rice
1 tablespoon soy sauce

METHOD
1. In a wok or frying pan over medium heat, heat 1 tablespoon oil. Add beaten eggs, swirling pan to coat base evenly with egg. Cook until eggs set, 1–2 minutes, then turn out of pan onto a board and let cool. Roll up omelet and slice into thin strips. Set aside.
2. In wok or pan over a high heat, heat remaining 2 tablespoons oil. Add scallions, garlic, ginger and celery, and stirfry for 2 minutes.
3. Add barbecued pork, shrimp, peas, omelet strips and rice, and stir-fry until heated through, about 5 minutes.
4. Add soy sauce and stir-fry until well combined. Serve hot.

HINTS
- Chinese barbecued pork is available from Asian food stores, markets, barbecue stores and restaurants. Substitute with cooked chicken meat in recipe; or replace with chopped bacon or ham, and add with scallions.
- Substitute barbecued pork with cooked shrimp (prawns) and add 8 oz (250 g) chopped Chinese vegetables such as bok choy or Chinese broccoli.

Lentil and bacon stew

SERVES 4

INGREDIENTS
1 tablespoon olive oil
1 onion, chopped
2 cloves garlic, crushed (see page 16)
2 slices thick-cut bacon, rind removed and chopped
1 small red chili pepper, seeds removed and chopped (see page 18)
   (optional)
1 cup (7 oz/220 g) red lentils, rinsed
1 medium potato, peeled and chopped
1 medium carrot, peeled and chopped
6 cups (48 fl oz/1.5 L) Chicken Stock (see page 154)
1 can (14 oz/425 g) crushed tomatoes
2 tablespoons chopped fresh flat-leaf (Italian) parsley leaves
2 tablespoons lemon juice
sea salt and freshly ground black pepper
crusty bread, for serving

METHOD
1. In a large saucepan over medium heat, heat oil. Add onion, garlic, bacon and chili, if using, and cook, stirring, until onion softens, 1–2 minutes.
2. Add lentils, potato, carrot and stock, and stir. Bring to a boil, reduce heat to low and simmer, uncovered, until lentils and vegetables are tender, 25–30 minutes.
3. Remove pan from heat. Working in batches, ladle stew into a food processor and process until smooth.
4. Return stew to saucepan over low heat and add tomatoes. Cook, uncovered and stirring occasionally, for 10 minutes.
5. Add parsley and lemon juice, and extra stock if soup is too thick. Season to taste with sea salt and black pepper. Serve with crusty bread.

Lentil patties

SERVES 4

INGREDIENTS

½ cup (3½ oz/100 g) red lentils

8 oz (250 g) sweet potato or yam (kumara), peeled and chopped into small cubes

1 carrot, peeled and cut into small cubes

1 teaspoon ground cumin

½ teaspoon ground coriander

2 cups (16 fl oz/500 ml) water

1 cup (2 oz/60 g) fresh bread crumbs

2 tablespoons chopped fresh flat-leaf (Italian) parsley leaves

2 tablespoons chopped fresh mint leaves

½ cup (2½ oz/75 g) all-purpose (plain) flour

1 cup (4 oz/125 g) dried bread crumbs

1 egg, beaten

2 tablespoons milk

3 tablespoons olive oil, for frying

lemon wedges, for serving

½ cup (4 fl oz/125 ml) Basic Mayonnaise (see page 82) or plain (natural) yogurt, for serving

METHOD

1. In a large saucepan over high heat, combine lentils, sweet potato, carrot, cumin, coriander and water. Bring to a boil, then reduce heat to low. Cover and simmer, stirring occasionally, until mixture thickens, 20–25 minutes. Remove pan from heat and let cool completely.

2. Add fresh bread crumbs, parsley and mint to lentil mixture. Mix well and refrigerate for 30 minutes.

3. Place flour and dried bread crumbs on separate plates. In a small bowl, combine egg and milk.

4. Using wet hands, divide lentil mixture into 4 portions and shape each into a patty. Coat each in flour, dip into egg and milk mixture, then coat in dried bread crumbs. Place on a plate and refrigerate for 30 minutes.

5. In a nonstick frying pan over medium heat, heat oil. Working in batches, cook lentil patties until golden on both sides, about 3 minutes each side. Remove from pan using a slotted spoon, and set aside on paper towels.

6. Serve lentil patties warm, with lemon wedges and mayonnaise or yogurt on the side.

Pad Thai noodles

SERVES 4

INGREDIENTS
8 oz (250 g) dried flat rice noodles
3 tablespoons vegetable oil
2 cloves garlic, crushed (see page 16)
1–2 small fresh red chili peppers, seeds removed and finely chopped
   (see page 18) (optional)
1 lb (500 g) skinless chicken breast fillet, cut into thin slices
3 tablespoons lemon juice
2 tablespoons fish sauce
1 tablespoon brown sugar
3 scallions (shallots/spring onions), sliced
2 eggs, beaten
1 cup (3 oz/90 g) bean sprouts, rinsed and drained
⅓ cup (½ oz/15 g) fresh cilantro (fresh coriander) leaves
¼ cup (1½ oz/45 g) roasted unsalted peanuts, chopped, for serving
4 lemon wedges, for serving

METHOD
1. Place noodles in a heatproof bowl and cover with boiling water. Let soak until softened, 10–15 minutes. Drain and rinse in cold water.
2. In a wok or nonstick frying pan over medium heat, heat oil. Add garlic, chili and chicken, and stir-fry until golden and tender, 3–4 minutes.
3. In a small bowl, combine lemon juice, fish sauce and brown sugar. Add to pan, and stir to combine.
4. Add drained noodles and scallions, and stir-fry for 3 minutes.
5. Push noodle mixture to one side of pan. Add beaten eggs to other side of pan and cook, without stirring, until partially set. Then stir egg gently until scrambled, before stirring to combine egg with noodles.
6. Add bean sprouts and cilantro to pan, and cook, stirring, until heated through, about 1 minute.
7. Transfer to individual plates, sprinkle each with peanuts and top with a lemon wedge. Serve immediately.

VARIATION For vegetarian Pad Thai noodles, substitute chicken with the same quantity of firm tofu, cut into cubes; add tofu with noodles in recipe.

Tomato and tuna risotto

SERVES 4

INGREDIENTS
4 cups (32 fl oz/1 L) Vegetable Stock (see page 155)
1½ cups (12 fl oz/375 ml) tomato puree
2 tablespoons olive oil
2 onions, chopped
2 cloves garlic, crushed (see page 16)
2 cups (14 oz/425 g) Arborio rice
1 can (12 oz/375 g) tuna in olive oil, drained and flaked
3 tablespoons chopped fresh basil leaves
½ cup (2 oz/60 g) grated Parmesan cheese
sea salt and freshly ground black pepper

METHOD
1. In a medium-sized saucepan over medium heat, heat stock and tomato puree. Bring to a boil, then reduce heat to low and let simmer.
2. In a medium-sized heavy-based saucepan over medium heat, heat oil. Add onions and garlic, and cook until onion softens, about 1 minute.
3. Add rice and cook, stirring, until translucent, about 2 minutes.
4. Slowly add 1 cup (8 fl oz/250 ml) hot stock, and stir constantly until absorbed, about 6–8 minutes.
5. Continue adding stock a cupful at a time until rice is soft and creamy, 20–25 minutes in total. Rice grains should be firm but tender.
6. Remove pan from heat, and fold in tuna, basil and Parmesan cheese. Cover and let stand 5 minutes before serving.
7. Season with sea salt and black pepper. Spoon into warmed serving bowls (see page 21) and serve immediately.

Vegetables

I've always loved my vegetables, but these days, a trip to the greengrocer or local market is a wondrous experience. Sweet aromas and colors abound, and the choice is inspiring. Who can walk away without bags and boxes full of produce?

It's not just the great range and availability of vegetables that makes them so popular. Like our ancestors who prized vegetables for their freshness and health-giving qualities, we realize that vegetables are very good for us. They are low in calories, and contain little or no cholesterol, yet are packed with vital nutrients. They are also economical, and in cooking they are extremely versatile.

You can serve vegetables as sides, simply cooked to take advantage of their unique flavors, or in main dishes that bring out their earthy richness and complexity. They combine well with almost all other foods—meat, poultry, fish, rice, noodles and grains—and may even be used in cakes and desserts.

As consumers we've come to expect most vegetables to be available year-round, but it's still best to enjoy them in season. If you know when vegetables are at the peak of their season, you can take advantage of better quality and lower prices. A good greengrocer will offer a "year-round" range as well as fruit and vegetables in season, and helpful advice! Better still, choose organic produce—you'll be amazed at the difference in taste, let alone the health benefits.

Purchasing vegetables

Try to choose blemish-free vegetables, with firm skin and a good color in most cases; remember some organic produce may have natural blemishes.

If possible, only purchase the amount you can use within 2–3 days to ensure you are eating the freshest vegetables at their best.

Storing vegetables

For best storage, many vegetables require a humid atmosphere, which is not normally available to householders: your refrigerator is the best substitute.

Most vegetables should be washed, drained and dried with paper towels, then placed into loose-fitting plastic bags. Place them in the lower compartments or vegetable crisper of your refrigerator. Mushrooms are exceptions and should not be washed but simply placed in a paper bag in the refrigerator.

Some vegetables, such as pumpkin or butternut squash, potatoes, garlic and onions, are best stored, unwashed, in a cool dark, well-ventilated cupboard or pantry. Some people believe that storing onions in the refrigerator will prevent you from crying when cutting them.

Vegetable cooking methods

How to blanch vegetables

Blanching is a method that partly cooks the vegetables, enhancing their natural vibrant colors and flavors. Vegetables, such as broccoli florets, green beans and asparagus, may be blanched before adding to salads.

1. Half-fill a medium-sized saucepan with water and bring to a boil over high heat.
2. Place vegetables in boiling water and cook only until their color becomes more brilliant, about 1 minute.
3. Using a slotted spoon, quickly remove vegetables from pan and plunge immediately into a large bowl of ice water to stop the cooking process.
4. Let vegetables cool completely in water, then drain well using a colander or sieve.

How to barbecue or pan grill vegetables

Barbecued or pan grilled vegetables are delicious served hot with meat, chicken or fish that has been cooked the same way. Or marinate the cooked vegetables in jars with olive oil and serve cold, such as in salads. Bell peppers (capsicums), zucchini (courgettes), onions and eggplants (aubergines) are just a few of the suitable vegetables.

1. Preheat barbecue or grill pan to very hot. Do not oil cooking plate, as this causes lots of smoke!
2. Cut vegetables into thick uniform slices and brush with olive oil.
3. Place vegetables onto barbecue or grill pan and cook until golden on both sides, 1–2 minutes.
4. Remove vegetables from barbecue or grill pan and serve hot, or let cool.

How to mash vegetables

Mashing is a great way to reinvent leftover cooked vegetables. What was cooked pumpkin one night can become creamy pumpkin mash the next night! While mashing cooked vegetables can be done in a food processor, they do become gluey and starchy, so I prefer to use the following method.

1. Boil vegetables until just tender, then drain well and return to warm saucepan.

2. Add 1–2 tablespoons milk or light (single) cream or a little extra virgin olive oil to cooked vegetables (this will help thin consistency of mash). Alternatively, add 1–2 tablespoons butter (this adds flavor without thinning the mash).

3. Using a vegetable masher, fork or whisk, mash vegetables until smooth and light. Season with plenty of sea salt and freshly ground black pepper to taste.

4. Spoon onto warmed serving plates (see page 21) and serve immediately.

How to puree vegetables

You can puree cooked vegetables in the food processor or use a sieve and wooden spoon or a food mill. The fine texture of pureed vegetables pairs well with barbecued, pan grilled, broiled (grilled) or roasted meat, chicken and fish. Try pumpkin or butternut squash, carrot or parsnip.

1. Boil vegetables until just tender then drain well.

2. Place cooked vegetables in a food processor and add 1–2 tablespoons butter, milk, light (single) cream or extra virgin olive oil. Process until smooth and thick. Alternatively, place vegetables in sieve and, using a wooden spoon, press through sieve, or use a food mill; then stir in butter, milk, cream or olive oil.

3. Season with plenty of sea salt and freshly ground black pepper to taste. Serve immediately.

HINT Do not puree cooked potatoes as they will become gluey.

How to roast vegetables

Many vegetables may be roasted with delicious results—potatoes, eggplants (aubergines), carrots, onions, pumpkins or butternut squashes, sweet potatoes or yams (kumara), beets (beetroot), parsnips and turnips, to name just some of the possibilities. Vegetables for roasting need minimal preparation: just a good wash under cold running water will suffice for most. Peeling is a matter of choice, but rarely necessary for young vegetables.

1. Preheat oven to 350°F (180°C/Gas 4). Grease a large roasting pan.

2. Cut vegetables into similar-sized pieces to ensure even cooking.

3. Place vegetable pieces in a single layer in a roasting pan. Sprinkle with sea salt and freshly ground black pepper, and drizzle with extra virgin olive oil.

4. Roast until golden and tender, 20–30 minutes depending on type, turning vegetables twice during cooking time.

5. Remove from oven and serve hot, with butter or a drizzle of extra virgin olive oil or balsamic vinegar, if desired.

How to stir-fry vegetables

This is a quick and easy method of cooking many vegetables, though starchy vegetables like potatoes are not suitable for stir-frying. It is important when stir-frying to have all the ingredients prepared before you start cooking: cut vegetables into similar-sized pieces to ensure even cooking, and measure any sauces you will need.

1. Heat a wok or deep nonstick frying pan over high heat until very hot, then add oil.
2. Add vegetables and other ingredients, as directed in recipe. Cook, stirring and tossing gently with a wooden spoon or spatula, until vegetables are brightly colored, 3–5 minutes.
3. Add flavorings like oyster and soy sauces at the end of cooking. Serve immediately for best flavor and texture.

HINT A wok is best for stir-frying, as the sloping sides make it easy to toss and turn food during cooking. If unavailable, use a deep, nonstick frying pan. Make sure the wok or pan is very hot before anything is added.

How to boil or steam vegetables

These are the most common cooking methods for vegetables, and also the most frequently misused! Overcooking by boiling too often leaves vegetables looking tired and limp, drained of their natural color, taste and nutrients. Yet, when correctly done, boiled vegetables are bright and crisp, packed with goodness and flavor.

Steaming is a gentle cooking process that preserves the natural texture, flavor and nutrient value of vegetables to a very high degree. For steaming, you will need a wok or saucepan with metal or bamboo steamer and lid.

To boil vegetables:

1. Fill a saucepan with enough water to cover vegetables, add salt to taste, and bring to a boil over high heat.
2. Cut vegetables into similar-sized pieces to ensure even cooking.
3. Add vegetables, and boil, uncovered, until just cooked; for root or hard vegetables reduce heat to medium–low and simmer until soft (see Quick Reference Guide, page 121).
4. Using a slotted spoon, quickly remove cooked vegetables and transfer to colander or sieve to drain (do not let green vegetables remain in boiling water longer than needed, as they will overcook).
5. If desired, return vegetables to warm saucepan and add 1 tablespoon butter or drizzle with extra virgin olive oil or lemon juice, and toss to combine.

To steam vegetables:
1. Cut vegetables into similar-sized pieces to ensure even cooking.
2. Half-fill a medium-sized saucepan or wok with water (steamer should not touch water) and bring to a boil over high heat.
3. Arrange vegetable pieces in steamer. Carefully place steamer over boiling water in pan or wok. Cover and steam until vegetables are tender, adding more water to pan or wok if necessary (see Quick Reference Guide, opposite). Caution: When removing lid of steamer, tilt it away from you to avoid burning from the steam.
4. Remove steamer from pan or wok, then remove vegetables using tongs. If desired, return vegetables to warm saucepan and add 1 tablespoon butter, or drizzle with extra virgin olive oil or lemon juice, and toss to combine.

HINTS

- When boiling vegetables, the cooking time greatly determines how much salt to add: as a guide, the longer the cooking time, the less salt is needed. Do not add salt to vegetables before steaming: instead, season just before serving.
- Cutting vegetable pieces the same size will ensure they cook evenly and are all ready at the same time; however, do not chop too finely, as too much of the vegetable's surface area will be exposed to water and cause excessive loss of nutrients and flavor.
- Fragile vegetables like asparagus should not be drained in a colander after boiling. Instead, use a slotted spoon to carefully remove from saucepan and let drain on paper towels. Drizzle with melted butter, olive oil, dressing or sauce just before serving.
- Traditionally, Hollandaise Sauce (see page 123) is served over hot boiled or steamed vegetables such as asparagus, broccoli, artichokes and cauliflower. Easily made in a food processor or blender, hollandaise sauce is best when warm, so prepare it just before serving.
- For a delicious change, drizzle salad dressing (see pages 80–81) over steamed or boiled vegetables before serving. Remember to shake the dressing before use.

Quick reference guide to boiling and steaming vegetables

This guide gives boiling and steaming instructions for specific vegetables. Cooking times, starting when water returns to a boil after vegetables are added, are approximate and depend on the vegetable variety, size and age. Smaller, younger vegetables cook more quickly than larger, older ones.

Test for doneness by piercing thickest part of vegetable with a sharp knife or skewer: it should be tender. Or simply taste a piece to check if it is cooked to your liking.

- **Asparagus**—In a saucepan with enough salted boiling water to cover, simmer gently for 5–8 minutes. Steam for about 10 minutes.
- **Bok choy**—In a saucepan of boiling water over high heat, boil for 1–2 minutes. Steam for 2–3 minutes.
- **Broccoli florets**—In a large saucepan with enough salted boiling water to cover, boil over high heat for about 5 minutes. Steam for 8–10 minutes.
- **Carrots**—In a saucepan with enough salted boiling water to cover, simmer gently for 5–10 minutes (older, thicker carrots will take longer). Steam for about 15 minutes.
- **Cauliflower florets**—In a large saucepan with enough salted boiling water to cover, simmer gently over medium–low heat for 3–5 minutes. Steam for 15 minutes.
- **Corn, ear (cob)**—In a large saucepan with enough salted boiling water to cover, boil over high heat for 6–8 minutes. Steam for 10–15 minutes.
- **Green beans**—In a large saucepan with enough salted boiling water to cover, boil whole beans for 2–5 minutes (sliced beans will cook more quickly). Steam whole beans for 5–10 minutes.
- **Peas, shelled**—In a saucepan with enough salted boiling water to cover, boil for 2–6 minutes. Steam for 5–10 minutes.
- **Potatoes**—There are two ways to boil potatoes; cooking times depend on size and variety. Method 1: Place in a large saucepan, cover with cold water, and bring to a boil over high heat. Reduce heat to medium and simmer, uncovered, for 10–15 minutes. Method 2: In a large saucepan with enough salted boiling water to cover, simmer for 10–15 minutes. Steam baby new potatoes, in their skin, for 20–25 minutes.
- **Pumpkin**—In a large saucepan with enough salted boiling water to cover, simmer gently over medium–low heat for 10–15 minutes. Steam for 10–20 minutes.
- **Snow peas (mange-tout)**—Add to a saucepan of salted boiling water and remove as soon as water returns to a boil. Steam for 1–2 minutes.
- **Spinach**—In a large saucepan with enough salted boiling water to cover, boil for 1–2 minutes, pushing leaves under water with a wooden spoon. Steam for about 2 minutes.

Asparagus with easy hollandaise sauce

Serve this dish as a vegetable accompaniment, or simply top with a poached egg and plenty of freshly ground black pepper for a special starter or lunch.

SERVES 4 AS A SIDE

INGREDIENTS

For easy hollandaise sauce
6 oz (180 g) butter
4 egg yolks
2 tablespoons lemon juice
sea salt and freshly ground black pepper

¾ lb. (375 g) fresh asparagus, about 2 bunches

METHOD
1. To make sauce: In a small saucepan over low heat, melt butter.
2. Place egg yolks in a blender or food processor, and blend for 20 seconds.
3. With motor running, gradually add hot butter in a steady stream. Blend until thick and creamy.
4. Add lemon juice and salt and pepper to taste, and blend to combine. Transfer sauce to a serving pitcher.
5. Cut woody ends from asparagus (see page 17), and trim ends using a vegetable peeler.
6. Fill a medium-sized saucepan two-thirds full with water and bring to a boil over high heat. Add asparagus and cook, uncovered, until bright green and tender, about 5 minutes. Remove from pan and drain on paper towels.
7. Arrange asparagus on serving plates and pour hollandaise sauce over. Serve immediately.

HINTS
- If hollandaise sauce becomes too thick, transfer sauce to a mixing bowl and whisk in a few drops of warm water, stock or cream.
- If sauce is too thin, place 1 teaspoon lemon juice and 1 tablespoon sauce in a separate bowl and whisk until thick, then gradually add remaining sauce to lemon juice mixture.
- If sauce curdles, it is usually because butter was added too quickly or because the mixture was overbeaten. To save a curdled sauce, transfer to

a mixing bowl then place the bowl in a larger bowl of ice water. Gradually whisk in a few drops of ice water then whisk well until sauce blends together.

Classic hollandaise sauce

Hollandaise sauce originated in France, and is traditionally made by hand—a skill which all apprentice chefs must learn in their first years. If you have a blender or food processor, and you've not made this sauce before, I suggest you start with the Easy Hollandaise Sauce (see opposite).

Hollandaise sauce, whether classic or easy, is delicious served over vegetables such as broccoli, artichokes and cauliflower, or over panfried or broiled (grilled) steak, chicken or fish, and poached eggs.

SERVES 4 AS A SAUCE

INGREDIENTS
3 tablespoons white wine vinegar
1 tablespoon water
6 whole black peppercorns
3 egg yolks
6½ oz (200 g) butter, cut into small cubes
juice of ½ lemon
sea salt and freshly ground black pepper to taste

METHOD
1. In a small saucepan over low heat, combine vinegar, water and peppercorns. Simmer until reduced to 1 tablespoon of liquid, then strain and set aside.
2. Place a small heatproof bowl over a saucepan half-filled with water; do not let base of bowl touch water. Place saucepan over medium heat. Add egg yolks and reduced vinegar mixture to bowl.
3. Using a balloon whisk, whisk egg mixture over simmering water until thick and creamy, 5–6 minutes.
4. Remove saucepan from heat, leaving bowl in place over water. Gradually add butter cubes, whisking well between each addition, until all butter is added and sauce is thick and creamy.
5. Stir in lemon juice and salt and pepper to taste. Serve warm.

Cauliflower au gratin

This is a quick and easy version of a vegetable classic. Serve it as an accompaniment with broiled (grilled) or roasted meats.

SERVES 4 AS A SIDE

INGREDIENTS
1 lb (500 g) cauliflower
2 tablespoons butter
1 tablespoon all-purpose (plain) flour
½ cup (4 fl oz/125 ml) milk
¼ cup (2 fl oz/60 ml) light (single) cream
⅓ cup (1½ oz/45 g) grated cheddar cheese
sea salt and freshly ground black pepper
2 tablespoons grated cheddar cheese, extra

METHOD
1. Cut cauliflower into medium-sized florets.
2. Half-fill a wok or saucepan with water and bring to a boil.
3. Arrange cauliflower in steamer, cover and place steamer over boiling water in wok or pan (steamer should not touch water). Cover and steam until cauliflower is tender, 10–15 minutes.
4. Meanwhile, in a small saucepan over medium heat, melt butter. Add flour and cook, stirring, until lightly golden, 1–2 minutes; do not let burn.
5. Remove pan from heat and gradually add milk and cream, stirring constantly.
6. Return pan to medium heat and cook, stirring, until sauce thickens, 3–4 minutes. Remove pan from heat. Add cheese and salt and pepper to taste, and stir to combine.
7. Preheat a broiler (grill). Grease a shallow baking pan and arrange cauliflower in base. Pour cheese sauce over evenly and sprinkle with extra 2 tablespoons grated cheese.
8. Broil (grill) until lightly golden, 1–2 minutes.
9. Spoon onto serving plates or serve from baking dish at table (make sure you protect table surface from hot dish).

HINT When purchasing fresh cauliflower, look for firm white compact heads without spots or bruises. Remove any leaves before storing in a plastic bag in the refrigerator.

Creamy mashed potato

For perfect mashing, choose the higher-starch varieties of potato such as Pontiac, King Edward, La Soda, Coliban, pink-eye, Nicola, russet or Sebago.

SERVES 4 AS A SIDE

INGREDIENTS
2 lb (1 kg) potatoes, peeled and cut into 1-in (2.5-cm) cubes
1½ oz (45 g) butter, softened
¾ cup (6 fl oz/180 ml) milk
sea salt to taste

METHOD
1. Place potatoes in a large saucepan and cover with cold water.
2. Bring to a boil over high heat, then reduce heat to medium–high and boil uncovered until tender, 8–10 minutes. Drain.
3. In a small saucepan over low heat, warm milk; do not boil.
4. Return drained potatoes to warm saucepan, and add butter and hot milk. Using a potato masher, mash until smooth and fluffy. (You may need to add a little more hot milk depending on potato variety.)
5. Season with salt to taste and serve.

HINTS
- Mash potatoes immediately after draining for best results.
- For a finer, smoother mash, press cooked potatoes through a fine sieve using a wooden spoon. Do not use a food processor, as they will become gluey and sticky.
- When buying potatoes, choose those with firm, unbroken skin. Avoid any with a green tinge, dark spots or green shoots.

Crispy roast potatoes

Varieties of potato most suitable for roasting include Desiree, Pontiac, fingerling (kipfler), Lasoda and pink-eye.

SERVES 4 AS A SIDE

INGREDIENTS
8 medium-size potatoes, peeled and halved horizontally
2 tablespoons olive oil
sea salt to taste

METHOD
1. Preheat oven to 400°F (200°C/Gas 6). Lightly brush a baking pan with olive oil.
2. Place potatoes in a medium-sized saucepan and cover with cold water. Bring to a boil, then reduce heat to medium–high and boil uncovered for 5 minutes. Drain well.
3. Pat potatoes dry with paper towels and let cool for 10 minutes.
4. Using the tines of a fork, gently rake rounded side of each potato half. Arrange potatoes in a single layer, cut side down, in baking pan. Brush potatoes with oil.
5. Bake until golden and crisp, 50–60 minutes, turning twice during cooking time.
6. Serve hot with sea salt to taste.

VARIATION Herbed Roast Potatoes
Sprinkle potatoes with 2 teaspoons chopped fresh rosemary leaves after brushing with oil.

Hash brown potatoes

Traditionally served for breakfast or brunch with broiled (grilled) bacon, hash browns also make a great vegetable side at lunch or dinner.

You will need 4 egg rings for this recipe; these are available from good kitchenware stores and some supermarkets. For best results, use a starchy potato variety like Sebago, russet or Desiree.

SERVES 4 AS A SIDE

INGREDIENTS
1 lb (500 g) potatoes, peeled
½ small onion, finely chopped (see page 16)
½ teaspoon sea salt
½ teaspoon freshly ground black pepper
1 tablespoon chopped fresh parsley leaves
2 tablespoons butter
1 tablespoon olive oil

METHOD
1. Place potatoes in a medium-sized saucepan and cover with cold water.
2. Bring to a boil, reduce heat to medium–high and boil, uncovered, until just cooked, 10–15 minutes (slightly longer if using russet potatoes). Drain well, then pat potatoes dry with paper towels and let cool.
3. Coarsely grate potatoes or chop into ½-in (12-mm) cubes. In a mixing bowl, combine potatoes, onion, salt, pepper and parsley, and mix well.
4. In a heavy-based frying pan over medium heat, melt butter. Add oil and stir to mix.
5. Grease 4 egg rings and place in pan. Spoon potato mix into egg rings, pressing down firmly to form flat cakes. Cook, pressing down on potato with a spatula, until golden underneath, about 6 minutes.
6. Carefully turn over and cook on other side until golden, about 4 minutes, pressing down firmly with spatula during cooking.
7. Remove from pan using a slotted spoon, then remove egg rings and drain hash browns on paper towels. Serve hot.

Guacamole

This famous avocado dip is delicious served with corn chips or crisp sticks of fresh carrot, celery and cucumber. Try it spread on sandwiches, or on warm whole-wheat (wholemeal) toast as a snack or brunch, or serve alongside broiled (grilled) or barbecued chicken.

SERVES 4 AS A DIP OR ACCOMPANIMENT

INGREDIENTS
2 ripe avocados
juice of 2 limes
1 small red chili pepper, seeds removed and finely chopped (optional) (see page 18)
2 tablespoons chopped fresh cilantro (fresh coriander) leaves
2 scallions (shallots/spring onions), finely chopped
sea salt and freshly ground black pepper

METHOD
1. Cut avocados in half, remove pit and roughly chop flesh (see page 18).
2. Place in a medium-sized bowl and, using a fork, mash until smooth.
3. Add lime juice, chili pepper, cilantro and scallions, and stir to combine. Season with salt and pepper to taste.
4. Serve immediately, as a dip or spread.

HINT Though technically a fruit, the avocado is mostly enjoyed as a vegetable, sliced, mashed or simply halved, with savory flavors such as chili, garlic, cilantro (coriander), bacon, chicken, or shrimp (prawns).

VARIATION With Garlic
Add 1 clove garlic, crushed (see page 16), with chili.

Oven-roasted vegetable salad

SERVES 4 AS A SIDE

INGREDIENTS
1 medium sweet potato or yam (kumara)
3 small beets (beetroot)
3 medium potatoes
2 large carrots
3 large zucchini (courgettes)
2 red bell peppers (capsicums), seeds removed (see page 18)
2 large red onions, cut into 8 wedges
4 cloves garlic, slivered
¼ cup (2 fl oz/60 ml) extra virgin olive oil
sea salt and freshly ground black pepper to taste
6 sprigs fresh rosemary
balsamic vinegar and extra virgin olive oil, for serving

METHOD
1. Preheat oven to 400°F (200°C/Gas 6). Grease a large roasting pan.
2. Rinse and dry vegetables; there is no need to peel them. Cut vegetables into uniform 2-in (5-cm) cubes.
3. Arrange vegetables, along with garlic, in a single layer in roasting pan. Drizzle with olive oil, and sprinkle with salt and pepper and then rosemary sprigs.
4. Bake until vegetables are golden and tender, 20–25 minutes, turning vegetables at least 3 times during cooking.
5. Remove from oven and toss to mix. Transfer to a serving bowl and serve vegetables warm, drizzled with balsamic vinegar and olive oil to taste.

HINT When purchasing, choose well-shaped zucchini (courgettes) with firm glossy skin and good color.

Potato, ham and cheese bake

The best varieties of potato to use for this family favorite are Desiree, Sebago or Coliban. Bake this together with roast chicken or beef, and serve as a side, or for a winter lunch with crusty bread.

SERVES 6 AS A SIDE

INGREDIENTS
2½ lb (1.25 kg) potatoes, peeled
½ onion, finely chopped (see page 16)
6½ oz (200 g) leg ham, chopped
1 cup (8 fl oz/250 ml) milk
1 cup (8 fl oz/250 ml) light (single) cream
sea salt and freshly ground black pepper
½ cup (2 oz/60 g) grated Parmesan cheese

METHOD
1. Preheat oven to 350°F (180°C/Gas 4). Grease a 6-cup (48-fl oz/1.5-L) baking dish.
2. Using a sharp knife, Japanese vegetable slicer or mandoline, slice potatoes very thinly, then pat dry with paper towels.
3. Arrange one-fourth of potatoes in a layer on base of baking dish. Spread one-third of onion and ham on top of potatoes.
4. Repeat layers of potato and ham and onion twice, then finish with a potato layer.
5. In a small saucepan, combine milk and cream together then warm over low heat; do not let boil. Season with salt and pepper to taste.
6. Pour cream mixture evenly over potato, cover baking dish with aluminum foil and bake for 30 minutes.
7. Remove aluminum foil and bake, uncovered, for a further 20 minutes.
8. Sprinkle top with cheese and bake, uncovered, until golden, a further 20 minutes.
9. Remove from oven and let stand 15 minutes. Cut into squares to serve.

Ratatouille

This hearty vegetable dish is ideal served alongside broiled (grilled), barbecued or roasted lamb. Or serve with a bowl of hot buttered noodles for a filling vegetarian meal.

SERVES 4 AS A SIDE

INGREDIENTS
8 oz (250 g) eggplant (aubergine), cut into 1¼-in (3-cm) cubes
salt
3 tablespoons olive oil
2 onions, sliced
2 cloves garlic, crushed (see page 16)
2 red bell peppers (capsicums), seeds removed, cut into 1-in (2.5-cm) cubes
1 lb (500 g) ripe tomatoes, peeled, seeds removed and roughly chopped
    (see page 17)
8 oz (250 g) zucchini (courgettes), thickly sliced
2 tablespoons chopped fresh flat-leaf (Italian) parsley leaves
sea salt and freshly ground black pepper

METHOD
1. Place eggplant on a plate lined with paper towels, sprinkle liberally with salt and let stand for 20 minutes.
2. Transfer eggplant to a colander and rinse well under cold running water. Pat dry with paper towels.
3. In a large heavy-based frying pan over medium heat, heat oil. Add onions and garlic, and cook, stirring, until onions soften and brown slightly, about 2 minutes.
4. Add eggplant and bell peppers, and cook, stirring, until vegetables soften, about 5 minutes.
5. Add tomatoes and zucchini, and stir to combine. Reduce heat to low, cover and cook until vegetables are tender, about 20 minutes.
6. Remove from heat using a slotted spoon, stir in parsley and season with salt and pepper to taste. Serve hot.

HINTS
- Eggplants (aubergines) are not usually peeled for cooking. However, to extract any bitter juices, sprinkle them with salt, then rinse before using.
- When buying eggplants, choose those with shiny, smooth and blemish-free skin. They should also feel heavy for their size. Store eggplants in the vegetable compartment of your refrigerator for up to 3 days.

Slow-roasted tomatoes

These are heavenly in so many ways—at breakfast as a side to scrambled eggs, pureed into deliciously rich tomato sauce, served warm as a salad or accompaniment, in sandwiches, or to top off a homemade pizza.

SERVES 4–6 AS A SIDE

INGREDIENTS
2 lb (1 kg) plum (Roma) tomatoes
4 sprigs fresh thyme
sea salt and freshly ground black pepper
¼ cup (2 fl oz/60 ml) extra virgin olive oil

METHOD
1. Preheat oven to 300°F (150°C/Gas 2). Line 2 baking sheets with parchment (baking) paper.
2. Cut tomatoes in half lengthwise. Arrange, cut side up, in a single layer on baking sheets.
3. Sprinkle with thyme. Then sprinkle liberally with salt and pepper.
4. Drizzle with olive oil and bake until tomatoes are shriveled and lightly golden, about 1½ hours.
5. Turn off oven and let tomatoes cool in oven.
6. Serve at room temperature as a side.

HINT To store cooked tomatoes, arrange in an airtight glass jar or container with lid. Pour in enough olive oil to completely cover tomatoes and seal jar. Store in refrigerator for up to 14 days. Once tomatoes are eaten, use remaining oil for dressings, marinating or basting foods before barbecuing or broiling (grilling).

VARIATIONS
- Add 4 cloves garlic, roughly chopped, or 4 large red chili peppers, halved lengthwise, to tomatoes before roasting.
- Substitute thyme with fresh rosemary.

Stir-fried Asian vegetables

Visit your local Asian supermarket or grocery and you'll find garden-fresh vegetables, as well as other Asian ingredients, at great prices. Remember to prepare all your stir-fry ingredients before you start cooking, and cut them in uniform pieces to ensure even cooking.

SERVES 4 AS A LIGHT MEAL

INGREDIENTS

2 tablespoons vegetable oil
2 onions, cut into 8 wedges
2 cloves garlic, crushed (see page 16)
2 teaspoons peeled and grated fresh ginger
1 bunch Chinese broccoli, about 13 oz (400 g), trimmed and
    cut into 2-in (5-cm) lengths
4 oz (125 g) snow peas (mange-tout), trimmed and sliced crosswise
1 red bell pepper (capsicum), seeds removed and sliced (see page 18)
1 cup (6 oz/180 g) canned baby corn, drained
1 bunch bok choy, about 13 oz (400 g), trimmed and cut into 2-in (5-cm)
    lengths
2 tablespoons oyster sauce
2 tablespoons Vegetable Stock (see page 155)
1 tablespoon soy sauce
steamed rice (see page 106), for serving

METHOD

1. In a wok or frying pan over medium heat, heat oil. Add onions, garlic and ginger, and stir-fry until onion softens, 1–2 minutes.
2. Add Chinese broccoli, snow peas, bell pepper, corn and bok choy. Stir-fry until vegetables are tender-crisp, 3–4 minutes.
3. In a small bowl, combine oyster sauce, stock and soy sauce. Add to pan and cook, stirring, until heated through, 1–2 minutes.
4. Serve hot, accompanied with steamed rice.

Stuffed mushrooms

This flavorsome dish may be served as a starter, snack, lunch or vegetable side to broiled (grilled) meats. Omit bacon if a vegetarian dish is desired.

SERVES 6 AS A STARTER OR SIDE

INGREDIENTS
6 large white (field) mushrooms, about 2½ oz (75 g) each
2 tablespoons olive oil
½ onion, finely chopped (see page 16)
2 cloves garlic, crushed (see page 16)
3 slices thick-cut bacon, rind removed and finely chopped
4 slices stale white bread
1 tablespoon chopped fresh thyme leaves or 1 teaspoon dried thyme
1 tablespoon chopped fresh flat-leaf (Italian) parsley leaves
sea salt and freshly ground black pepper
2 tablespoons olive oil, extra

METHOD
1. Preheat oven to 350°F (180°C/Gas 4). Grease a baking pan. Remove mushroom stems and finely chop (see page 19).
2. In a frying pan over medium heat, heat oil. Add onion, garlic and bacon, and cook, stirring, until bacon browns, about 3 minutes.
3. Add chopped mushroom stems and cook, stirring, until softened, about 2 minutes. Transfer stuffing mixture to a mixing bowl and let cool.
4. Remove crusts from bread and tear bread into pieces. Place in a food processor or blender and process until bread crumbs form.
5. Add bread crumbs, thyme and parsley to cooled stuffing, and mix until well combined. Season with salt and pepper to taste.
6. Arrange mushrooms, dark side up, on baking pan. Brush with extra 2 tablespoons oil. Spoon stuffing into each mushroom.
7. Bake mushrooms until golden, about 20 minutes. Serve immediately.

HINTS
• For a great brunch idea, serve each stuffed mushroom on a thick slice of toasted sourdough and drizzle with extra virgin olive oil.
• Store fresh mushrooms in a paper bag in the refrigerator.

VARIATION With Cheese
Sprinkle stuffed mushrooms with grated Parmesan cheese before baking.

Vegetable lasagna

SERVES 6

INGREDIENTS
2 medium eggplants (aubergines), about 1¼ lb (625 g) in total
salt
olive oil
2½ cups (1½ lb/750 g) ricotta cheese
½ cup (2 oz/60 g) grated Parmesan cheese
3 tablespoons chopped fresh flat-leaf (Italian) parsley leaves
3 tablespoons chopped fresh basil leaves
1 egg, beaten
sea salt and freshly ground black pepper to taste
11½ oz (350 g) fresh lasagna sheets
1 quantity Neapolitan Sauce (see page 101)
1 cup (4 oz/125 g) grated mozzarella cheese

METHOD
1. Grease a deep 12-in x 10-in (30-cm x 25-cm) baking pan or an 8-cup (64-fl oz/2-L) baking dish.
2. Cut eggplants in ½-in (12-mm) slices. Transfer to plate lined with paper towels, sprinkle with salt and let stand 30 minutes. Place in a colander and rinse well under cold running water. Pat dry with paper towels.
3. Preheat a grill pan or barbecue. Brush eggplant slices with olive oil on both sides. Grill eggplant until golden on both sides, about 5 minutes. Using a slotted spoon, remove from pan and drain on paper towels. Set aside.
4. In a medium-sized mixing bowl, combine ricotta and Parmesan cheeses, parsley, basil, egg, and season with salt and pepper. Mix until well combined.
5. Preheat oven to 350°F (180°C/Gas 4).
6. To assemble, arrange a layer of lasagna sheets over base of baking pan or dish. Spread half of cheese mixture over top. Cover with half of eggplant and spoon over half of sauce. Add another layer of lasagna sheets and spread remaining cheese mixture over top. Cover with remaining eggplant, then top with remaining sauce. Sprinkle top with mozzarella cheese.
7. Bake until golden on top, 40–45 minutes. Remove from oven and let stand 15 minutes. Cut into squares to serve. Serve with Green Salad (see page 86) and Herb-Garlic Bread (see page 92).

HINT Substitute eggplant with grilled or barbecued zucchini (courgettes) and/or red bell peppers (capsicums).

Cakes, cookies and desserts

One of the best things about being able to cook the basics is sweets! Whether it's a delicate sponge cake with lashings of whipped cream or peanut butter cookies to satisfy the family, a sweet treat always tastes so much better when made at home. Of course, when you cook cakes and the like, you have to eat them.

Desserts, cakes, cookies and sweets aren't as difficult as many people think. The secret is in the preparation: have eggs at room temperature, sift dry ingredients like flour, grease baking pans, and preheat the oven when necessary. And don't overwork batter or dough, as the results will often be tough.

In this chapter you'll find basic recipes for some of my favorite sweets, including classic cakes, like chocolate and carrot, comforting cookies, and impressive desserts. Some of these are ideal for special occasions, while others may be enjoyed daily! Best of all, the recipes are easy—even for the most inexperienced cook—and use commonly available ingredients. It's definitely worth the effort!

Cooking methods

How to beat

Beating combines and aerates ingredients. It can be done by hand using a wooden spoon or with an electric mixer, depending on recipe instructions. Using a food processor will not add air to a mixture; it will instead blend it to a smooth paste.

1. Place ingredients in mixing bowl.
2. Using a wooden spoon or an electric mixer, as directed in recipe, beat until light and fluffy.

HINTS

- Beat egg whites in a clean and dry bowl to achieve maximum volume (see page 20).
- Beat cream in a chilled bowl and do not overbeat or the cream will curdle (see page 20).

How to cream

Creaming is the process of beating together ingredients, such as butter and sugar, until they become pale and creamy in appearance, and light and aerated in texture. This is best done using an electric mixer. Use good-quality butter that has softened slightly but is not melted.
1. Place ingredients in mixing bowl.
2. Using an electric mixer, beat until pale and creamy, scraping down sides of bowl occasionally with a spatula.

How to fold

Folding is a gentle process for mixing ingredients together. It combines the ingredients without losing the aeration of the mixture.
1. Place ingredients in a mixing bowl, as directed in recipe.
2. Using a large metal spoon, fold ingredients together, using a slow cutting action. Do not stir or beat when folding.

How to whisk

Whisking is a process that combines ingredients and also adds air to the mixture. Whisking can be done by hand using a wire whisk or with an electric mixer.
1. Place ingredients in mixing bowl.
2. Using a wire whisk or an electric mixer, as directed in recipe, whisk until light and fluffy.

How to grease baking pans

1. In a small saucepan over low heat, melt a little butter.
2. Using a glazing brush, brush melted butter over base and sides of baking pans or cake pans, as required.

HINT You can line the baking pan with a piece of parchment (baking) paper in place of greasing.

How to sift

Many dry ingredients, such as flour, confectioners' (icing) sugar, baking powder and cocoa are sifted to remove lumps and to add air.
1. Place measured ingredients into a flour sifter or fine wire or nylon sieve over a mixing bowl.
2. Shake or tap sifter or sieve so that flour sifts into bowl.

Apple pie

SERVES 8–10

INGREDIENTS
For pastry
2 cups (10 oz/300 g) all-purpose (plain) flour
5 oz (150 g) chilled unsalted butter, cut into small pieces
2 tablespoons superfine (caster) sugar
2 tablespoons ice water
1 egg yolk

For filling
4 oz (125 g) butter
1 cup (7 oz/220 g) packed brown sugar
2 tablespoons lemon juice
2 tablespoons finely grated lemon zest
5 tart green apples, peeled, cored and cut into eighths

METHOD
1. To make pastry, place flour, butter and sugar in food processor and process until mixture resembles fine bread crumbs. In a separate bowl lightly whisk together water and egg yolk and add to flour mixture. Process just until mixture starts to come together. Remove from processor and gently knead so mixture forms mass. Pat into disk shape, wrap in plastic wrap and refrigerate 30 minutes.
2. Divide pastry into two pieces, one twice the size of the other. Refrigerate smaller piece. Roll out larger piece on lightly floured surface to fit 10-inch (25-cm) tart pan with removable bottom. Line pan with pastry, trim edges and refrigerate 30 minutes.
3. Preheat oven to 400°F (200°C/Gas 6). Line pastry with parchment (baking paper) and cover with dried beans or rice. Bake 20 minutes, then remove beans or rice and paper. Return to oven and bake until golden, about 5 minutes. Set aside to cool slightly.
4. To make filling, melt butter with sugar in large frying pan over a low heat, stirring to dissolve sugar. Stir in lemon juice and zest. Add apples and simmer until soft, about 20 minutes. Set aside to cool.
5. Using slotted spoon, transfer apples to pastry shell, allowing as much liquid as possible to drain from each spoonful.
6. Preheat oven to 350°F (180°C/Gas 4). Roll out remaining pastry and cut into strips. Place over apple mixture in lattice pattern. Bake until pastry is crisp and golden, about 20 minutes. Serve warm.

Banana cake

SERVES 6

INGREDIENTS
4 oz (125 g) butter, softened
1⅓ cups (10 oz/300 g) superfine (caster) sugar
2 eggs, lightly beaten
2 small ripe bananas, mashed
2 cups (10 oz/300 g) all-purpose (plain) flour
1 teaspoon baking soda (bicarbonate of soda)
1 teaspoon ground cinnamon
¼ teaspoon ground allspice
½ cup (4 fl oz/125 ml) milk
1 teaspoon lemon juice

For topping
3 tablespoons rolled oats
3 tablespoons self-rising (self-raising) flour
2 tablespoons brown sugar
2 teaspoons ground cinnamon
3 tablespoons butter, softened

METHOD
1. Preheat oven to 350°F (180°C/Gas 4). Grease an 8-in (20-cm) deep round cake pan. Cut a round piece of parchment (baking) paper to fit base of pan, then line pan with paper.
2. In a medium-sized bowl, combine butter and sugar. Using an electric mixer, beat together until light and fluffy.
3. Add eggs and mashed banana and using mixer, mix well.
4. In a separate bowl, sift together flour, baking soda, cinnamon and allspice. In a small bowl, combine milk and lemon juice.
5. Fold flour mixture alternately with milk into butter mixture, finishing with flour. Spoon evenly into cake pan.
6. To make topping: In a small bowl, combine oats, flour, sugar and cinnamon. Add butter and using your fingertips, rub in butter until mixture resembles coarse bread crumbs.
7. Sprinkle topping mix evenly over cake mixture.
8. Bake until a skewer inserted into center of cake comes out clean, about 1 hour. Cool cake in pan.
9. Turn out cake onto a plate. Cut into slices to serve.

Basic baked cheesecake

This is a mouthwatering, creamy cheesecake that will have everyone coming back for more. I prefer the rich flavors of the continental cream cheese and ricotta cheese available from good delicatessens, though you can substitute with the supermarket varieties.

SERVES 6

INGREDIENTS
8 oz (250 g) plain whole-wheat (wholemeal) cookies
4 oz (125 g) butter, melted
12 oz (375 g) cream cheese
1¾ cups (14 oz/425 g) ricotta cheese
4 eggs
1⅓ cups (10 oz/300 g) superfine (caster) sugar
1 tablespoon cornstarch (cornflour)
1 tablespoon grated lemon zest
¼ cup (2 fl oz/60 ml) lemon juice

METHOD
1. Preheat oven to 300°F (150°C/Gas 2). Grease an 8-in (20-cm) round springform cake pan. Cut a piece of parchment (baking) paper to fit base of pan, then line pan with paper.
2. Place cookies into a food processor and process until crushed. Add melted butter and process until well combined.
3. Firmly press crumb mix into base of pan and refrigerate.
4. To make filling, place cream cheese and ricotta cheese into clean food processor. Process until smooth. Add eggs, sugar, cornstarch, lemon zest and juice. Process until well combined.
5. Pour filling evenly over prepared cookie base and bake until set, about 1 hour and 10 minutes.
6. Turn off oven and let cheesecake stand in oven for 2 hours to cool. Then refrigerate overnight.
7. Cut into wedges and serve.

Basic cookies

MAKES ABOUT 24

INGREDIENTS
4 oz (125 g) butter, softened
½ cup (3½ oz/110 g) superfine (caster) sugar
¼ cup (2 fl oz/60 ml) milk
¼ teaspoon vanilla extract (essence)
1½ cups (7½ oz/235 g) self-rising (self-raising) flour
½ cup (2 oz/60 g) custard powder or vanilla pudding powder

METHOD
1. Preheat oven to 400°F (200°C/Gas 6). Grease or line 2 baking sheets with parchment (baking) paper
2. In a medium-sized mixing bowl, combine butter and sugar. Using an electric mixer, beat together until light and creamy.
3. Add milk and vanilla extract, and beat until well combined.
4. In a separate bowl, sift flour and custard powder together. Add flour mixture to butter mixture and using a metal spoon or knife, mix to a soft dough.
5. To shape cookies, scoop up about 1 tablespoon of the mixture, roll into a ball between your palms and place on baking sheet, leaving about 2 in (5 cm) between the balls to allow room for spreading during baking.
6. Using the back of a fork, press down gently on each ball.
7. Bake until golden, about 15 minutes. Remove from oven and let cool on baking sheets.

HINT Store cooled cookies in an airtight container for up to 7 days.

VARIATION Press a whole almond or walnut on top of each cookie instead of pressing with a fork before baking.

Basic butter cake

SERVES 6

INGREDIENTS
4 oz (125 g) butter, softened
¾ cup (6 oz/185 g) superfine (caster) sugar
1 teaspoon vanilla extract (essence)
2 eggs
2 cups (10 oz/300 g) self-rising (self-raising) flour
pinch salt
½ cup (4 fl oz/125 ml) milk
⅓ cup (3 oz/90 g) raspberry jam
½ cup (4 fl oz/125 ml) light (single) cream or heavy (double) cream,
   whipped (see page 20)

METHOD
1. Preheat oven to 350°F (180°C/Gas 4). Grease two 8-in (20-cm) round cake pans. Cut two pieces of parchment (baking) paper to fit bases of pans, then line pans with paper.
2. In a mixing bowl, combine butter, sugar and vanilla. Using an electric mixer, beat together until light and creamy.
3. Add eggs, one at a time, beating well after each addition.
4. In a separate bowl, sift flour and salt together. Using a large metal spoon, gently fold flour mixture alternately with milk into butter mixture, finishing with flour.
5. Spoon evenly into cake pans. Bake until a skewer inserted into center of cake comes out clean, 25–30 minutes.
6. Remove from oven and turn out cakes onto wire racks to cool.
7. Spread one cooled cake with jam then spoon over cream. Spread base of remaining cake with jam, and place on top of cream.
8. Using a serrated knife, cut into wedges to serve.

HINT Dust top of finished cake with sifted confectioners' (icing) sugar, if desired.

VARIATIONS
• Raisin and Spice Butter Cake: Fold in ⅔ cup (4 oz/125 g) golden raisins (sultanas) and 1 teaspoon ground mixed spice (or ¼ teaspoon each ground cinnamon, allspice, cloves, ginger, and nutmeg) with flour.
• Lemon Butter Cake: Replace vanilla extract (essence) with grated zest of 1 lemon and 2 teaspoons lemon juice.

Bread and butter pudding

Originally invented in Britain as a way of using leftover bread, this pudding is now made by choice! It is cooked in a "water bath" in the oven, a gentle method of cooking that prevents the eggs in the custard from curdling.

SERVES 4

INGREDIENTS
3 eggs
2 tablespoons superfine (caster) sugar
1 teaspoon vanilla extract (essence)
2½ cups (20 fl oz/625 ml) milk
8 slices stale white bread
2 tablespoons butter, softened
1 tablespoon golden raisins (sultanas)
¼ teaspoon ground nutmeg

METHOD
1. Preheat oven to 350°F (180°C/Gas 4). Using a glazing brush, grease a 4-cup (32-fl oz/1 L) baking dish with melted butter.
2. In a medium-sized bowl, combine eggs, sugar and vanilla extract. Using a whisk or fork, blend together. Add milk and mix until well combined.
3. Remove crusts from bread slices using a serrated bread knife, then spread one side of each slice with butter. Cut each slice in half, to form triangles.
4. Arrange half of bread slices, butter side down, in base of baking dish. Sprinkle golden raisins over top.
5. Pour half of custard mix evenly over top and let stand 5 minutes.
6. Top with remaining bread slices, butter side down. Pour remaining custard evenly over top and sprinkle with nutmeg.
7. To prepare a water bath, place pudding dish into a larger baking dish and carefully add boiling water to reach halfway up sides of pudding dish. Bake until golden and set, about 40 minutes.
8. Remove pudding from oven and water bath and let stand 10 minutes. Serve warm or chilled with cream if desired.

HINT Cover cooled pudding with plastic wrap and refrigerate for 1–2 days.

VARIATIONS
• Spread bread slices with strawberry jam after buttering.
• Substitute white bread with raisin bread or brioche.

Carrot cake

SERVES 6

INGREDIENTS

1 cup (5 oz/150 g) all-purpose (plain) flour

1 teaspoon baking powder

1 teaspoon baking soda (bicarbonate of soda)

½ teaspoon ground mixed spice, or pinch each ground cinnamon allspice, cloves, ginger, and nutmeg

½ teaspoon ground cinnamon

¼ teaspoon salt

½ cup (3½ oz/100 g) superfine (caster) sugar

2 eggs, beaten

½ cup (4 fl oz/125 ml) vegetable oil

⅓ cup (2 oz/60 g) golden raisins (sultanas)

1½ cups (6 oz/180 g) grated carrot

2 teaspoons confectioners' (icing) sugar, sifted, for serving

METHOD

1. Preheat oven to 325°F (170°C/Gas 3). Grease an 8½-in x 4½-in (21.5-cm x 11-cm) loaf pan and line with parchment (baking) paper.
2. In a large mixing bowl, sift flour, baking powder, baking soda, mixed spice, cinnamon and salt. Stir in sugar.
3. Add eggs and oil, and mix until well combined.
4. Add sultanas and carrot, and stir to combine. Pour cake mixture into prepared pan.
5. Bake until a skewer inserted into center of cake comes out clean, about 1 hour and 10 minutes.
6. Remove from oven, and turn out cake onto a wire rack to cool.
7. Dust with sifted confectioners' sugar and cut into slices to serve.

HINT Once cooled, carrot cake may be stored in an airtight container at room temperature for up to 4 days.

Chocolate cake

SERVES 6

INGREDIENTS
6½ oz (200 g) butter, softened
1¼ cups (9 oz/280 g) superfine (caster) sugar
⅓ cup (1 oz/30 g) cocoa, sifted
3 eggs, separated (see page 19)
1¼ cups (6½ oz/210 g) self-rising (self-raising) flour
⅔ cup (4 oz/125 g) all-purpose (plain) flour
¾ cup (6 fl oz/180 ml) milk
½ cup (4 fl oz/125 ml) light (single) cream or heavy (double) cream,
    whipped (see page 20)
1 cup (4 oz/125 g) fresh strawberries, hulled and sliced (see page 17)
1 tablespoon confectioners' (icing) sugar, sifted

METHOD
1. Preheat oven to 350°F (180°C/Gas 4). Grease two 8-in (20-cm) deep round cake pans. Cut two pieces of parchment (baking) paper to fit bases of pans, then line pans with paper.
2. In a medium-sized bowl, combine butter and sugar. Using an electric mixer, beat until light and creamy.
3. Add sifted cocoa and egg yolks, and beat until well combined.
4. In a separate bowl, sift flours together. Fold into butter mixture with milk.
5. Place egg whites in a clean bowl and, using an electric mixer, beat until soft peaks form (see page 20). Using a metal spoon, gently fold into cake mixture. Pour cake mixture evenly into cake pans.
6. Bake until cake top springs back when lightly touched, about 1¼ hours.
7. Remove from oven, and turn out cakes onto wire racks to cool.
8. Spread one cooled cake with whipped cream and arrange strawberries evenly over cream. Top with remaining cake. Dust top with sifted confectioners' sugar.
9. Using a serrated knife, cut into wedges to serve.

Chocolate mousse

SERVES 4

INGREDIENTS
3 eggs
6½ oz (200 g) good-quality dark chocolate, chopped
¾ cup (6 fl oz/180 ml) light (single) cream
½ cup (4 fl oz/125 ml) heavy (double) cream, for serving

METHOD
1. Separate eggs (see page 19). Place egg yolks in a small bowl and lightly beat with a fork. Place egg white in a clean mixing bowl and set aside.
2. Place chocolate and light cream in top of a double boiler or in a heatproof bowl. Place over simmering water, and stir until chocolate melts and mixture is smooth and glossy, about 5 minutes.
3. Remove from heat and let cool for 5 minutes, then mix in egg yolks.
4. Using an electric mixer or whisk, beat egg whites until soft peaks form (see page 20). Using metal spoon or spatula, gently fold egg whites, in two batches, into chocolate mixture.
5. Spoon mousse into 6 serving glasses or ramekins. Cover and refrigerate until firm, about 4 hours or overnight.
6. Before serving, top each with a dollop of heavy cream.

HINT Chocolate mousse will keep for 2 days in the refrigerator.

Peanut butter cookies

Who can resist peanut butter in a cookie? These childhood favorites will be popular with both adults and children.

MAKES ABOUT 20

INGREDIENTS
4 oz (125 g) butter, softened
grated zest of 1 orange
⅓ cup (2½ oz/75 g) superfine (caster) sugar
⅓ cup (2½ oz/75 g) firmly packed brown sugar
⅓ cup (3 oz/90 g) crunchy peanut butter
1¼ cups (6½ oz/210 g) all-purpose (plain) flour
1 teaspoon baking soda (bicarbonate of soda)

METHOD
1. Preheat oven to 350°F (180°C/Gas 4). Lightly grease or line two baking sheets with parchment (baking) paper.
2. In a medium-sized mixing bowl, combine butter, orange zest, sugars and peanut butter. Using an electric mixer, beat until well combined.
3. In a separate bowl, sift together flour and baking soda. Using a wooden spoon, stir flour and soda into butter mixture, and mix to a stiff dough.
4. To shape cookies, scoop up about 1 heaping teaspoon of the mixture, roll into a ball between your palms and place on baking sheet, leaving about 2 in (5 cm) between the balls to allow room for spreading during baking.
5. Using the back of a fork, press down gently on each ball.
6. Bake until golden, about 15 minutes. Remove from oven and let cool on baking sheets.

HINTS
- Store cooled cookies in an airtight container for up to 7 days.
- By letting the cookies cool on the baking sheets, you will ensure they're crunchy and crisp.

VARIATION With Chocolate
Once the cookies are cooled, you can drizzle them with melted dark chocolate or dip half of each cookie in melted milk chocolate (see page 20). Place on a wire rack and let rest until chocolate is firm.

Pikelets

You can enjoy these small, sweet Scottish pancakes for breakfast, brunch or afternoon tea. Serve with your favorite raspberry jam or just simply buttered and hot!

MAKES ABOUT 12

INGREDIENTS
1 cup (5 oz/150 g) self-rising (self-raising) flour
pinch salt
¼ teaspoon baking soda (bicarbonate of soda)
2 tablespoons superfine (caster) sugar
1 egg, lightly beaten
½ cup (4 fl oz/125 ml) milk
½ cup (4 fl oz/125 ml) buttermilk
2 tablespoons butter, melted
extra melted butter, for frying
½ cup (5 oz/150 g) raspberry jam
½ cup (4 fl oz/125 ml) light (single) cream or heavy (double) cream, whipped (see page 20)

METHOD
1. In a medium-sized bowl, sift flour, salt and baking soda. Add sugar and stir.
2. In a pitcher or mixing bowl, combine egg, milk, buttermilk and butter, and mix well. Add to flour mixture and mix just until combined.
3. Heat a nonstick frying pan over medium–low heat. Lightly grease with extra melted butter.
4. Working in batches of 3 or 4 at a time, place about 1 tablespoon batter into pan for each pikelet, leaving space for spreading. Cook pikelets until golden underneath and bubbles form on top, 1–2 minutes. Then turn over pikelets using a spatula and cook until golden on other side, a further 1 minute. Transfer to a plate and set aside. Repeat until all batter is cooked.
5. Serve warm or cold with jam and whipped cream.

Rice custard, baked

This baked rice custard is a traditional favorite, originally made to use up leftover cooked rice. If cooking rice for this recipe, you'll need 2 tablespoons raw short-grain white rice to yield the ½ cup cooked rice required.

SERVES 4

INGREDIENTS
3 eggs, lightly beaten
⅓ cup (2½ oz/75 g) superfine (caster) sugar
1 teaspoon vanilla extract (essence)
2½ cups (20 fl oz/625 ml) milk
½ cup (2½ oz/75 g) cooked short-grain white rice
¼ cup (1½ oz/45 g) golden raisins (sultanas)
½ teaspoon ground nutmeg

METHOD
1. Preheat oven to 350°F (180°C/Gas 4). Grease a 4-cup (32-fl oz/1-L) baking dish.
2. In a medium-sized bowl, combine eggs, sugar, vanilla and milk, and mix using a whisk.
3. Add cooked rice and golden raisins, and using a wooden spoon, stir until combined.
4. Pour rice mixture evenly into baking dish and sprinkle top with nutmeg.
5. To prepare a water bath, place pudding dish into a large baking dish and carefully add boiling water to baking dish to reach halfway up sides of pudding dish. Bake until golden and set, about 45 minutes.
6. Serve warm or chilled.

HINT Once cooled, the custard can be covered with plastic wrap and stored in the refrigerator for 1–2 days.

Scones with jam and cream

The secret to great scones is to add nearly all the liquid at once—a soft sticky dough will yield light scones. Also, handle the dough lightly, as overkneading makes the scones tough.

MAKES 12

INGREDIENTS
2 cups (10 oz/300 g) all-purpose (plain) flour
pinch salt
2 tablespoons butter, cut into cubes
½ cup (4 fl oz/125 ml) milk
½ cup (4 fl oz/125 ml) water
½ cup (5 oz/150 g) strawberry jam
½ cup (4 fl oz/125 ml) light (single) cream or heavy (double) cream, whipped (see page 20)

METHOD
1. Preheat oven 450°F (230°C/Gas 8). Line a baking sheet with parchment (baking) paper.
2. In a medium-sized bowl, sift together flour and salt. Add butter and using your fingertips, rub butter into flour mixture until mixture resembles bread crumbs.
3. In a small bowl, combine milk and water. Make a well in center of flour mixture and add nearly all of milk and water mixture. Using a butter knife, mix to a soft dough, adding remaining milk and water only if needed.
4. Turn out dough onto a floured board. Knead lightly together, then roll or press to a thickness of ¾ in (2 cm).
5. Using a floured 2-in (5-cm) cookie cutter, cut dough into rounds. Place rounds onto prepared baking sheet.
6. Bake until golden, about 12 minutes.
7. Remove from oven and transfer scones to a wire rack to cool.
8. Serve scones at room temperature. Cut or tear scones in half to serve, spread with jam and top with a spoonful of whipped cream.

HINT Scones are best eaten on the day they are baked.

Sponge cake

A light and delicate sponge cake is easy—just make sure the eggs are at room temperature, lots of air is beaten into them (you will need an electric mixer for this), and you bake the cake immediately.

SERVES 6

INGREDIENTS
1¼ cups (6½ oz/200 g) all-purpose (plain) flour
6 eggs
¾ cup (6 oz/180 g) superfine (caster) sugar
2 oz (60 g) butter, melted
⅓ cup (3 oz/90 g) raspberry jam
confectioners' (icing) sugar, sifted, for dusting

METHOD
1. Preheat oven to 350°F (180°C/Gas 4). Brush two 8-in (20-cm) round cake pans with melted butter and dust with flour. Cut two pieces of parchment (baking) paper to fit base of pans, then line pans with paper.
2. Sift flour three times, then set aside.
3. In a medium-sized mixing bowl, combine eggs and sugar. Using an electric mixer, beat until thick and pale in color, about 8 minutes.
4. Sift flour over egg mixture and gently fold through using a large metal spoon. Fold in melted butter.
5. Pour evenly into cake pans and immediately bake until lightly golden and center of sponge springs back when lightly touched with your finger, 20–25 minutes.
6. Turn out cakes onto wire racks to cool.
7. Spread jam over one cake. Top with remaining cake and dust with confectioners' sugar.

VARIATIONS
• Add whipped cream (see page 20), spread over jam, before sandwiching sponge cakes together.
• Add whipped cream and fresh sliced strawberries (see Chocolate Cake, page 145), instead of jam, before sandwiching sponge cakes together.

Stocks and marinades

Nothing beats the flavor of homemade stock. It brings an incomparable richness to dishes, and can be the difference between good food and great food. While it takes a little effort to make your own stock, the result is worth it—and homemade stock is easy to store in the refrigerator or freezer, so it can be as convenient as something off the shelf.

Marinating is one of the simplest ways to add flavor to meat, fish and chicken before cooking, and you can create marinades to suit your taste. Marinating also enhances the moisture level of food, keeping it juicy and more succulent, and making it easier to cook.

Storing homemade stock

Once cooled, stock may be kept in an airtight container in the refrigerator for up to 5 days and frozen for up to 2 months. Freezing stock in small quantities, for example 1 cup (8 fl oz/250 ml) or less, makes it very convenient for use in soups, gravies and sauces.

1. To freeze, place a plastic freezer bag inside a plastic tub or container, opening the bag and folding the top edge over the rim of the container.
2. Measure stock and place in bag.
3. Freeze until hard, then remove bag with frozen stock from the container.
4. Seal, label and date the bag.

Marinating foods

You can marinate foods for just a few minutes or up to several hours or even overnight. The longer the marinating time, the stronger the flavor will be, so don't marinate delicate-flavored foods like fish for too long. Because many marinades include an acid-based ingredient like citrus juice or wine, it is best to use a glass or ceramic bowl for marinating.

1. Place marinade ingredients in a screw-top jar, and shake to mix.
2. Brush marinade over food. Cover and refrigerate for 15 minutes or more (except for fish, which should be marinated for 15 minutes at most). Drain food and cook as desired.
3. Marinades may be kept sealed in a jar in the refrigerator for up to 4 days.

Beef stock

Use this stock in soups, sauces and gravies.

MAKES 10 CUPS (80 FL OZ/2.5 L)

INGREDIENTS
4 lb (2 kg) beef bones
2 onions, roughly chopped
2 celery stalks, roughly chopped
2 carrots, roughly chopped
3 whole black peppercorns
2 bay leaves
3 sprigs fresh parsley
16 cups (130 fl oz/4 L) water

METHOD
1. In a large saucepan over high heat, combine all ingredients.
2. Bring to a boil. Using a slotted spoon, remove any scum from surface of stock.
3. Reduce heat to medium–low and simmer gently, uncovered, for 2 hours.
4. Carefully strain stock using a metal sieve. Discard bones and vegetables.
5. Let stock cool to room temperature. Remove any fat that sets on surface.
6. Store in a sealed container in refrigerator for up to 5 days or freeze (see opposite).

Chicken stock

Use this stock in soups, sauces and gravies.

MAKES ABOUT 8 CUPS (64 FL OZ/2 L)

INGREDIENTS
4 lb (2 kg) chicken bones
2 onions, roughly chopped
2 celery stalks, roughly chopped
2 carrots, roughly chopped
3 whole black peppercorns
2 bay leaves
3 stalks fresh parsley
16 cups (130 fl oz/4 L) water

METHOD
1. In a large saucepan over high heat, combine all ingredients.
2. Bring to a boil and using a slotted spoon, remove any scum from surface of stock.
3. Reduce heat to medium–low and simmer gently, uncovered, for 2 hours.
4. Carefully strain stock using a metal sieve. Discard chicken and vegetables.
5. Let stock cool to room temperature. Remove any fat that sets on surface.
6. Store in a sealed container in the refrigerator for up to 5 days or freeze (see page 152).

HINTS
- You can purchase bags of chicken bones especially for making stock at speciality poultry stores and some butcher shops.
- For a richer-flavored chicken stock, place chicken bones in greased roasting pan and roast in a preheated 350°F (180°C/Gas 4) oven until golden, about 30 minutes. Drain off any fat before using roasted bones in recipe.

Vegetable stock

Use this stock in soups, sauces and gravies.

MAKES ABOUT 8 CUPS (64 FL OZ/2 L)

INGREDIENTS
1 onion, roughly chopped
1 leek, white part only, chopped
2 celery stalks, roughly chopped
2 parsnips, roughly chopped
2 carrots, roughly chopped
6 whole black peppercorns
2 bay leaves
3 sprigs fresh parsley
16 cups (130 fl oz/4 L) water

METHOD
1. In a large saucepan over high heat, combine all ingredients.
2. Bring to a boil. Using a slotted spoon, remove any scum from surface of stock.
3. Reduce heat to medium–low and simmer gently, uncovered, for 2 hours.
4. Carefully strain stock using a metal sieve. Discard vegetables.
5. Let stock cool to room temperature.
6. Store in a sealed container in the refrigerator for up to 5 days or freeze (see page 152).

Basic marinades

The following recipes make enough for 1 lb (500 g) meat or fish. Place ingredients in a screw-top jar, and shake to mix (see page 152).

BEEF MARINADE
4 cloves garlic, crushed (see page 16)
⅓ cup (3 fl oz/90 ml) red wine
2 tablespoons olive oil
plenty of freshly ground black pepper

CHICKEN MARINADE
2 cloves garlic, crushed (see page 16)
1 teaspoon chopped fresh thyme leaves
3 tablespoons dry white wine or lemon juice
¼ cup (2 fl oz/60 ml) olive oil

FISH MARINADE
2 teaspoons peeled and grated fresh ginger
1 tablespoon finely chopped fresh cilantro (fresh coriander) leaves
3 tablespoons lemon or lime juice
¼ cup (2 fl oz/60 ml) olive oil
1 tablespoon Thai sweet chili sauce (optional)

LAMB MARINADE
4 cloves garlic, crushed (see page 16)
½ cup (4 fl oz/125 ml) lemon juice
⅓ cup (3 fl oz/90 ml) olive oil
1 teaspoon ground paprika
2 teaspoons chopped fresh rosemary or oregano leaves
plenty of freshly ground black pepper

Index

Guide to weights and measures

The conversions given in the recipes in this book are approximate. Whichever system you use, remember to follow it consistently, to ensure that the proportions are consistent throughout a recipe.

WEIGHTS

Imperial	Metric
1/3 oz	10 g
1/2 oz	15 g
3/4 oz	20 g
1 oz	30 g
2 oz	60 g
3 oz	90 g
4 oz (1/4 lb)	125 g
5 oz (1/3 lb)	150 g
6 oz	180 g
7 oz	220 g
8 oz (1/2 lb)	250 g
9 oz	280 g
10 oz	300 g
11 oz	330 g
12 oz (3/4 lb)	375 g
16 oz (1 lb)	500 g
2 lb	1 kg
3 lb	1.5 kg
4 lb	2 kg

OVEN TEMPERATURE GUIDE

The Celsius (°C) and Fahrenheit (°F) temperatures in this chart apply to most electric ovens. Decrease by 25°F or 10°C for a gas oven or refer to the manufacturer's temperature guide. For temperatures below 325°F (160°C), do not decrease the given temperature.

Oven description	°C	°F	Gas Mark
Cool	110	225	1/4
	130	250	1/2
Very slow	140	275	1
	150	300	2
Slow	170	325	3
Moderate	180	350	4
	190	375	5
Moderately hot	200	400	6
Fairly hot	220	425	7
Hot	230	450	8
Very hot	240	475	9
Extremely hot	250	500	10

USEFUL CONVERSIONS

1/4 teaspoon	1.25 ml
1/2 teaspoon	2.5 ml
1 teaspoon	5 ml
1 Australian tablespoon	20 ml (4 teaspoons)
1 UK/US tablespoon	15 ml (3 teaspoons)

BUTTER/SHORTENING

1 tablespoon	1/2 oz	15 g
1 1/2 tablespoons	3/4 oz	20 g
2 tablespoons	1 oz	30 g
3 tablespoons	1 1/2 oz	45 g

VOLUME

Imperial	Metric	Cup
1 fl oz	30 ml	
2 fl oz	60 ml	1/4
3 fl oz	90 ml	1/3
4 fl oz	125 ml	1/2
5 fl oz	150 ml	2/3
6 fl oz	180 ml	3/4
8 fl oz	250 ml	1
10 fl oz	300 ml	1 1/4
12 fl oz	375 ml	1 1/2
13 fl oz	400 ml	1 2/3
14 fl oz	440 ml	1 3/4
16 fl oz	500 ml	2
24 fl oz	750 ml	3
32 fl oz	1L	4